THE MEDIEVAL SOLDIER

15th Century Campaign Life
Recreated in Colour Photographs

Gerry Embleton
& John Howe

THE CROWOOD PRESS

Dedication

To Sophie, Samuel and Dana

This edition published by
The Crowood Press Ltd
Ramsbury, Marlborough
Wiltshire SN8 2HR

www.crowood.com

British Library Cataloguing-in-Publication Data
A catalogue record for this book is available from the British Library.

ISBN 978 1 85915 036 9

Designed by John Anastasio/Creative Line

Origination by Eray Scan Pte Ltd

Printed in Malaysia by Alden Press

Contents

Preface

An historian on history:

"I take delight in history, even in its most prosaic details, because they become poetical as they recede into the past. The poetry of history lies in the quasi-miraculous fact that once, on this earth, once, on this familiar spot of ground, walked other men and women, as actual as we are today, thinking their own thoughts, swayed by their own passions, but now all gone, one generation vanishing after another, gone as utterly as we ourselves shall shortly be gone like a ghost at cockcrow. This is the most familiar and certain fact about life, but it is also the most poetical, and the knowledge of it has never ceased to entrance me, and to throw a halo of poetry round the dullest record that Dryasdust can bring to light."

G. M. Trevelyan, 'Autobiography of an Historian'

Letter from a 15th century lady to her lord:
"For God's sake, if your brothers go over the sea, advise them as best you can for their safekeeping. For some of them are but young soldiers, and know full little what it means to be a soldier, and to endure as a soldier should do..."

Margaret Paston to Sir John Paston, 23 May 1475

History should be the most exciting of all subjects for study, since it is our own story - the story of everything we ever were, are and could be. It is little short of criminal that as frequently taught in our schools it is the dullest; seldom is an informed effort made to bring the past alive and make it relevant to our own lives. Nevertheless, in recent years thousands of people have turned to the re-creation of the past as a hobby, frequently finding in this pursuit of "living history" qualities that have been lost from our 20th century lives, opening up a window through which to glimpse their ancestors, and uncovering a mirror in which to see themselves more clearly.

The "Middle Ages" are generally reckoned by academics to have started in 1000 AD and to have ended shortly before 1500 - a period of five centuries. I do not believe that there is a period in recorded history (except, perhaps the years of the American Old West) about which more myths have been invented and more false impressions firmly planted in the public mind. This book is a modest attempt to bring one small part of the past closer, and to make it a little more real and understandable.

Enlisting help among the best of the "living history" enthusiasts, trying carefully to eliminate all modern objects and making certain items specially for these photographs, we have tried to bring alive here the world of the late 15th century soldier; and by doing so, we hope to awaken the reader to the simple fact that "history" was something that really happened to people very like ourselves. We chose this narrow scope the better to concentrate our efforts. All the work which went into this book was done by amateurs enjoying their hobby; like theatre, it requires dedication, huge effort, and considerable expense. The reward is the pure magic of those moments when it all works - just a few moments, when time itself seems to slip.

While we have been scrupulous in our choice of primary sources of information, it should always be remembered that those sources are arbitrary survivors, a completely unbalanced and random body of information selected by fate and time. For example, the illustrated chronicles of Tchachtlan and the Schillings afford us an amazingly rich glimpse at life in what is now Switzerland between 1470 and 1515; but English references for the same period are very sparse indeed. This does not mean that life in England was any less richly varied or less coloured by local custom and peculiarity - merely that less reference material has come down to us.

Archaeology helps us to build up the skeleton of an impression of 15th century life: the size of the people, the pots they cooked in, the buttons that fastened their clothing. Written accounts and contemporary illustrations tell us what went into the pots, and what colours they dyed their clothes. Careful reconstruction by serious "living history" students - what has been called "experimental archaeology" - can tell us how it felt to wear the clothes, and the smell and taste of the food in the pots.

An enormous amount of research over many years lies behind this book, which is a team effort assisted and encouraged by many scholars and museums. The books and documentary sources we have used are far too numerous to list here; whenever possible we have worked from copies of the original texts in French, German and English. However, the selected titles listed below are not too difficult to find, have been the very backbone of this book, and will take the reader far more deeply into the subject. We humbly acknowledge our debt to the authors.

Gerry Embleton
Onnens
May 1994

Further reading:
Philippe Aries & Georges Duby, *A History of Private Life* (1988, The Belknap Press of Harvard University Press)
Philippe Contamine, *La guerre au moyen age* (1980, Presses Universitaires de France)
David Edge & John M. Paddock, *Arms and Armour of the Medieval Knight* (1988, Defoe Publishing)
John Keegan, *The Face of Battle* (1976, Jonathan Cape)
Harry Künnel, *Alltag im Spätmittelalter* (1984, Editions Kaleidoskop)
Nicholas Michael, *Armies of Medieval Burgundy 1364-1477* (1983, Osprey Publishing Ltd.)
Volker Schmidtchen, *Kriegswesen in späten Mittelalter* (1990, VCH Verlagsgesellschaft mbH)
Robert D.Smith & Ruth Rhynas Brown, *Bombards, Mons Meg and her Sisters* (1989, Royal Armouries Monograph I, HM Tower of London)
Richard Vaughan, *Charles the Bold* (1973, Longmans Group Ltd.) [This, with Professor Vaughan's other three titles on the Burgundian dukes, is an absolute model of research and a pleasure to read. GAE]

15TH CENTURY EUROPE

R ather than attempt a broad description of this huge subject in so small a space, it seems more useful to sketch a few images in the hope of correcting the mythical popular picture - that of knights in castles, with nothing in between but a howling wilderness inhabited by wretched, starving peasants.

Wilderness there certainly was; many areas were much more heavily wooded than today, and some great forests limited all communication to a few narrow roads and waterways. But many areas had been cleared long centuries before, for Iron Age farmland and fuel; and landscapes of fields, lanes and villages were already ancient. Unchannelled rivers flooded their valleys in spring, and marshlands spread for hundreds of square miles; but canal-digging and reclamation by drainage had been in progress for centuries.

Today, in great valleys like that of the Rhone, we can still see castles perched along the ranges of hills marking the edges of the fertile flatlands, sitting astride and controlling the roads which skirted the river flood plains. In the 15th century many castles, villages and towns were spilling out from their original closely defended sites and sprawling along the fertile valleys; the population was growing in most parts of Europe. Some areas lay under cultivation much as they do today; here villages still occupy much the same sites, clustered around churches which have tolled out their bells over much the same landscapes for nearly a thousand years. Other regions were relatively much emptier in the 15th century than they are today, or indeed, had been a century before, and were haunted by overgrown ghost-villages; the continent was recovering from the Black Death, which had killed at least a third of the

Peasants return weary from the fields near the Chateau de Vufflens some time in the 1470s. Their lord must pay for his impressive new castle, built of brick in the latest Italian style; he has mortgaged his lands and borrowed heavily. It is not easy for the peasants to look to the future with any joy...

(Overleaf) In this year of grace 1474 exceptional weather promises the best grape harvest for years for these peasants picking in their vineyards near the castle of Aigle in Savoy, south-west of Lake Geneva. If God continues to bless them - and if the accursed "Germans" from Berne and the Valais cease their raids - then they will be able to buy more vines next year.
(Photos Philippe Krauer/L'Illustré)

population of most countries in 1348-50, but the recovery - like the plague-scourge, which had depopulated whole regions but passed others by - was uneven.

Trade routes were busy; at mountain passes and other chokepoints on the continent-wide road network wagons and pack-trains were slowed by nose-to-tail traffic jams. Everywhere there flowed the immense riches that fed the flourishing cities and courts, along ancient routes long established to carry the specific products of the different quarters of Europe .

The concept of "Europe" , however, did not exist in most 15th century minds. The village and the lands of its lord marked the horizons of most peoples' lives; the king was a remote power, near to God and set in his high place by God's will. Although the concept of the nation-state was becoming more firmly defined, all men and nations were united as members of Christendom, under the sway of the one Church.

Private letters and documents show that the normal hurly-burly of family life has never really changed, though in the 15th century social responsibilities and freedoms were more closely governed by local custom and the rule of the Church. Large extended families could be a bulwark against hard times and bad fortune. Writings and pictures suggest a richly stratified, vibrant society of hard toil and joyful celebration, living on the fragile balance between good and bad harvests, with an earthy vitality and a closeness to natural rhythms which we may legitimately envy without over-romanticism.

The other side of the coin was grimmer. Medieval man was always at the mercy of the powerful, and there was seldom hope of appeal or redress against arbitrary injustice. Brutal war could sweep across the land without warning. A ravaged or a failed harvest could mean literal starvation. Poor relief was a general Christian duty, and in places well-organised, but was never sufficient. If calamity and poverty struck, the lucky might be able to exist on the charity of a monastery or great hall. The beggar could be driven from one parish to another, whipped, branded or imprisoned. For those who stole to eat punishment was swift and cruel. Unless

lucky enough to find a place with relatives, in service, or with a religious order the maimed and blind, the destitute elderly, and the crippled soldier had little hope. *(Photo Claude Huyghens & Françoise Danrigal)*

While the Church might be universally acknowledged, however, she was not uniformly respected or obeyed. Her impotence in the face of the Black Death had shaken the confidence of many; in their despair some had given themselves over to fanatical cults. A more scholarly independence of thought was stirring among the tiny class of what we would today call "intellectuals"; many more were driven to cynicism by the worldly ways of the princes of the Church, and out in the countryside there were plenty of simple folk who still had one ear for the old gods. At times the Church could still show a tolerance which would become impossible after the Reformation began; at times she could crush doubters with ferocious cruelty.

The passage of the plague, striking down duke and ploughman alike, had affected many aspects of society. The reduced labour force of surviving peasants and craftsmen had rebelled against the former order of things, fighting for higher wages and new freedoms. There was cruelty, fear and gloom enough; but the survivors and their succeeding generations had a new vitality. Reminders of the fragility of earthly hopes were everywhere – death's image grinned from church walls, paintings and book plates; but life was for living while it lasted.

The 15th century world was violent at every level. Arguments quickly led to flying fists and drawn daggers. Apprentices fought students in the city streets with cudgels, even bows. Churchmen and townsfolk brawled, and teenage noblemen went at each other with steel. Few children can have grown up without seeing street fights, riots, duels, or local raids. In Switzerland, Germany, and in frontier regions of other countries armed raiding parties of 12-to-18-year-olds went out on holidays to steal cattle, or simply to terrify neighbouring villages; and some of the wilder young girls must have participated too. Many sports and entertainments were rough and callous by our standards; and holiday festivities and games frequently ended in spilt blood and broken heads.

For the most part the old feudal system was gone. Peasants were free to prosper if they could, and many did. There were relatively wealthy, as well as poor, at every level of the working and trading population – peasants, farmers, herders, shepherds, smiths, millers, small traders and carriers not excepted. Some of every class were on their way up: marrying off their children cunningly; buying up fields, an orchard, a hillside of vines; watching, planning and dealing. Others were on their way down, by ill-luck, sickness, slow-wittedness, lazyness, or the chance blows of the passing Riders–War, Pestilence and Famine.

Modern archaeological digs in peasant houses in France have yielded metal and pottery vessels, pewterware, keys, coins, and many other finds which paint a picture of a way of life little different from that of the 18th century. Analysis of diet, of animals kept and rents paid, of skeletons – often tall, with sound bones and good teeth – reinforce this impression. The villages visible in the backgrounds of "Gothic" paintings remained little changed for centuries; and a mid-19th century Suffolk, Vaudois, Provençale or Hessian village and its occupants had more in common with their 15th century ancestors than with their 20th century descendants.

(Right) At the stone sink in her kitchen window a woman washes wooden bowls and pottery plates. Her family are at work in the fields, and she will soon join them. Her husband owns two wagons; after years of struggle they have finally prospered enough to improve the stone house which they rent – but life is uncertain. A single bad harvest, a broken leg, might mean loss of their roof and the brink of the short slope to penury.

(Below) For this young widow life will be difficult – a year married, and her craftsman husband dead of plague. She could try to carry on his business: she knows his craft, has often helped him, and his guild is sympathetic. There is an eight-year-old apprentice, a cousin whose family is too large to support him. She has a two-room apartment, and is comfortable enough; but the future is precarious. It will be a lot easier if she remarries as soon as she can. *(Photos Gerry Embleton)*

A young bourgeois woman and her child enjoy an afternoon of calm, though not of idleness for her. She has a household to run, and she does so efficiently. She has married well; she is the second wife of a master craftsman, an important man in their town. She has been taught that submission, obedience, and constant attention will keep her husband happy (as he constantly reminds her). But he is an agreeable man; she married him when she was 14, and they have come a long way together. Now she sits in their good solid stone house, not new but comfortable. With her good management they will many their children well, and be secure enough in old age, God willing...
(Photo Philippe Krauer/ L'Illustré)

Town and City

Suffering the ravages of passing armies or oppressive rulers, countryman took up arms and fought against town, and worker and craftsman rebelled against burgher and merchant. Both peasant and townsman fought land-owning knight for greater independence; and the knight retaliated savagely against a tide which was slowly but inevitably eroding the last of his feudal rights.

In towns ever more conscious of their independent rights, regulations laid down that every man must turn out well-armed and equipped to protect the walls - and must either train himself to do so effectively, or pay another to do it in his place. Widows enjoying certain levels of property or business concerns had the same obligations, and sometimes even fought alongside the men.

With increasing frequency towns employed bands of professional soldiers - whose presence could be a mixed blessing. In their struggle for rights and immunities some towns amassed impressive arsenals; some of the independent cities acquired firearms, cannons and siege equipment that enabled them to defy princes and destroy castles. Self-interest led to intense rivalry, which vitalised civic pride. The Flemish cities defied their own Duke Charles of Burgundy; and it was a union of Strasbourg, Basle, Berne and others - rather than the machinations of the duke's fellow monarch, Louis XI of France - which destroyed Burgundy finally.

COSTUME

Basic male dress: a woollen coat or jacket worn over woollen doublet and hose laced together, over a linen shirt and drawers. An all-purpose knife and pouch were very commonly worn on a belt. *(Photo John Howe)*

The very word "costume" gets in the way of our attempt to imagine how our ancestors dressed. We would not refer to our everyday 20th century clothes as "costume". The medieval men and women who people 15th century paintings and manuscript illustrations did not dress up in impractical garments in order to pose. Except for ceremonies, fêtes and other special occasions they wore functional clothing, well made to last - even to hand down - suited to the work they did, the climate, and their own aesthetic preferences. Exactly the same may be said of the way we dress today (except for "well made to last"...).

Contemporary illustrations show a remarkable similarity in the dress worn throughout late 15th century Europe, but this impression is probably exaggerated by the scarcity of images of the middle and lower classes of society. The first records of clearly defined regional costumes appear in the 16th century, and show different styles for married and unmarried women, bourgeois and nobles, even within the same city. It seems most likely that such differences had long existed; it is in the very nature of human beings to advertise tribal, community, regional, national, political or religious loyalties in their dress and embellishments. There are tantalising glimpses of such practices in 15th century iconography, but much research remains to be done on this subject.

As a rule, people of all ranks seem to have dressed about the house in simple, old and comfortable clothes, keeping their best for venturing out or entertaining. Peasants, too, seem to have had holiday clothes - perhaps their wedding finery carefully put by or remade for festivals.

In parts of Italy, at least, partial undress or even nudity within the house was not considered shocking. Family life within the home could be very informal. People generally slept naked, and might strip to their chemise or take off their hose to settle down by the fireside.

One fact which cannot be over-emphasised is that in general the 15th century soldier was *not* a penniless serf. The knightly family's household soldiers were picked men, and retainers usually came from the humbler property-owning classes. They had to be well equipped in order to serve efficiently; most seem to have been well paid, at the level of skilled artisans, and household men were periodically supplied with new clothes, or cloth to be made up. There were, of course, exceptions, but most campaigns did not last long enough to reduce them to rags. In general, 15th century armies were nothing like the ragged gypsy hordes of the 17th century Thirty Years' War.

Given the traditional limitation of military operations to the months between seedtime and harvest, the chronicles record a surprising degree of effective winter campaigning - impossible without warm, weatherproof clothes and sturdy footwear. Woollen clothing worn in layers - doublet and hose, jacket, cloak and hood - give better protection than most modern man-made fibres (as the author can personally testify); and in extreme cold an overgown or "watching coat" was occasionally issued to such men as sentries.

Men of all classes wore the same basic garments, cloth and cut varying with their purse and their station in life:

Braies, breche

Underpants of simple cut, made short, with a slit or pouched front and drawstring waist, seem to have been usual. *The Book of Curtasye* of the reign of Henry VII of England (1485-) states

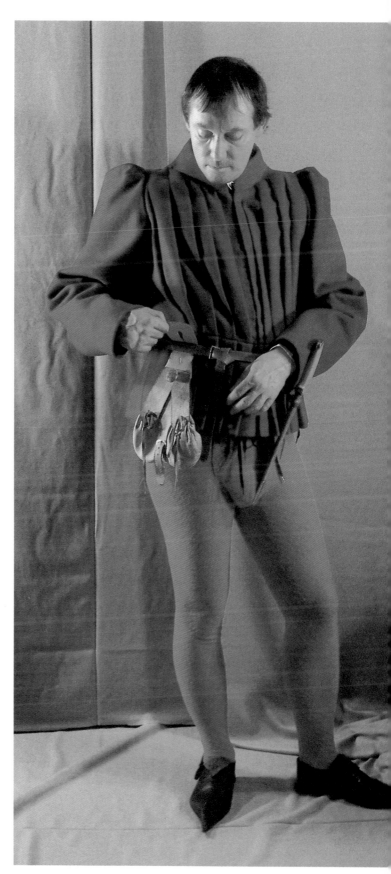

that the Chamberlain must provide "a clene sherte and breche" for his master upon waking.

Shirt

A simple T-shaped garment, which might be linen for a soldier, silk for a lord. It was cut long and very full, with a simple neck band or simply a slit for the head. The shirt rarely showed under formal dress.

Hose

The hose were originally separate, stocking-like legs; by the later 15th century they had become a tighter-fitting trouser-like garment made of very elastic wool or other flexible fabric, frequently made complete with feet, sometimes with simply a strap of material under the instep. Eyelets and "points" or laces were placed at intervals around the waist.

Doublet

A close-fitting jacket, with eyelets around the skirt; doublet and hose were laced together to support the hose.

Over the doublet were worn short coats of various styles and longer gowns, with many fashionable variations. Armour was usually worn over a specially reinforced arming-doublet; and a sleeveless, cutaway doublet was sometimes worn under the soldier's padded jack.

Hats were universally worn, of various simple shapes in woollen materials; "strawen hattes" were common in summer. Hoods coming well down over the shoulders - a most practical garment - were very popular. Overgowns of various kinds, and cloaks, were worn in cold weather, as were gloves or mittens, although these are rarely illustrated. ("Have here my myttens to put on they hands, other treasures I have none to present thee with...")

(Far left) Putting on the doublet over the linen shirt and woollen footed hose.

(Left) Lacing the doublet and hose together with "points". *(Photo John Howe)*

(Left below & right) Shoes were generally made inside out and then turned, so that the stitches were protected within the seams. Vegetable-tanned leathers, of a better quality than normally found today, were in general use. Most shoes were moccasin-style, low cut and without built-up heels; others were cut above the ankle.

The rougher the task, the tougher the shoe and the thicker the leather; reinforced soles or – more rarely – separate built-up soles and heels were sometimes added. Most peasants, and presumably footsoldiers, needed strong footwear. Shoes were fastened with points (laces), buckles, buttons, leather toggles, or sometimes wrap-around straps.

A large number of soldiers were mounted, and lighter shoes and boots, both short and long, were worn. A fashionable type were thigh-length boots with turn-down tops; these could be attached to the doublet skirt by a strap and point, or worn folded down – sometimes right down below the knee, so that the upper edge fell just above the instep.

While the toes of many shoes were fashionably pointed, round toes were also widespread – and in one document are in fact specified, for mounted archers in Burgundian service. We have found only one mention of shoe nails, which seems curious, since they were common in Roman times and certainly in use in 1515; perhaps they were limited to the heaviest types of boot?

"Pattens" or wooden-soled clogs **(below)** were popular with all classes in muddy weather. They lift the foot out of the wet, keep the sole warm, and are practical for town, farm and camp life – though not for a long march or for battle. *(Photos Gerry Embleton)*

Private possessions

A "book of housekeeping" of 1523 suggests that a good servant learn by heart a list of his master's possessions. With few exceptions this might as easily be a description of the equipment and personal belongings of a well-paid 15th century household archer: "Purse, dagger, cloak, night cap, kerchief, shoeing horn, wallet, shoes, spear, bag, hood, halter, saddle cloth, spurs, hat, horse comb, bow, arrows, sword, buckler, horn, leash, gloves, string, bracer, pen, paper, ink, parchment, red wax, pumice [eraser], books, penknife, comb, thimble, needle, thread, spare points, bodkin, knife, shoemaker's thread". The reader is also urged to "give thy horse meat, see he be shoed well, make merry, sing and thou can; take heed of thy gear, that thou lose none."

Daggers, knives and purses

Swords were rarely worn by civilians, and were frequently forbidden in towns; but daggers and knives were carried by most men. Tucked behind a bulging purse worn on the front of the belt like a sporran, they were a fashionable masculine symbol; carried horizontally on the back of the belt, they could be drawn swiftly and secretly. Every quarreler's weapon, they also formed part of ceremonial and travelling dress.

Most peasants, travellers and hunters carried general purpose knives; some were small, others resembled a large Bowie knife with miniature eating knives and other tools set in small sheaths on the scabbard. Soldiers carried daggers of many different sizes and shapes, but their eating knives and purses are rarely visible in period pictures. Money and personal possessions - even knives - were worn safely tucked away inside clothing or kit bags. Women are depicted with purses and small knives suspended between their outer and inner skirts. *(Photo left: John Howe)*

(Below left) Kidney-shaped purses were very popular with all ranks, and metal decorations were common: lead or pewter for the commoner, silver-plated or gilded for gentlemen like this household archer. *(Photo Gerry Embleton)*

(Below) A common form of single-edged dagger, with a rondel hilt, flanked by two typical eating/general purpose knives. *(Photo Gerry Embleton)*

WOMEN'S COSTUME

Basic costume consisted of a linen shirt, an underdress, an overdress, stockings and shoes. There is no evidence that underpants were worn.

The few pictorial references show the shirt (smock, chemise) cut loosely, reaching below the knee, usually white and very plain, with neither decoration nor drawstring at the neck. They were much more easily cleaned than the woollen dresses, and seem to have been washed and changed frequently. Purse, taste and circumstance dictated the quantity and quality of cloth used: generally speaking, the poorer the owner, the less cloth and the coarser the material.

The underdress (kirtle, cote) was a close-fitting, rather plain ankle-length garment, usually closed down the front, back, or sometimes the sides by laces. The neckline was usually wide but not too low,

showing little of the chemise. There were many subtle differences in shape. Sleeves were usually close-fitting and often short, with long false sleeves pinned on. This was the woman's everyday working dress. The elasticity of the woollen cloth, together with skillful tailoring, including pleats and darts, helped the more fashion-conscious achieve the desirable smooth fit.

The overdress (gown, robe, houppelande) was simply a slightly longer version of the underdress, often worn over and completely covering it. The underdress would perhaps be visible only at the neck, or if the skirts of the overdress were hitched up. Fuller styles were popular, falling in rich folds and frequently belted high above the waist. Wide belts were popular, of cloth woven like webbing or of leather patterned to resemble weaving. Heavier woollen or fur linings were used in cold weather by all but the very poor (cheap furs were available). Fashionable skirts were sometimes cut to trail on the ground, a style impossible for working women. *(Photos John Howe, Carlos Oliveira)*

Colours

Analysis of wool samples from Flemish tapestries in the Metropolitan Museum of Art, New York, was recently carried out at the Institut Royal du Patrimoine Artistique in Brussels. All the colours were made from three readily available vegetable dyestuffs: red from madder, the root of *rubia tinctorum*; yellow from weld, also known as *dyer's rocket*; and blue from woad, *isatis tinctoria*. A huge range of subtle tints can be achieved by combining two and sometimes three colours, and by varying the metallic mordents used to give permanence and richness. From these three plants can be made bright yellows, oranges and ochres, yellow-browns, olive, light and bright greens, deep blue-greens, blues from indigo to palest sky, crimson, mauve, purple, pinks, bright reds - even a good black, made with all three dyes and aluminium salts as a mordent.

Medieval dyers used many other substances, some rare and costly; but madder, weld and woad were common and relatively cheap. It is often said that certain colours were little used; but black, yellow, and the mauve-purple range including "murray" appear not infrequently in lively colours and contemporary illustrations of rich and not so rich alike.
(Photo Carlos Oliveira)

Headdress

Illustrations show that hair was normally grown long and plaited, and bound round the head or coiled over the ears; sometimes a single plait was worn, or the long hair tied at the nape. Women's hair was usually hidden; at some times and places it seems to have been fashionable, or the mark of the unmarried, for young girls to show theirs. Women at home or at work would have been more relaxed, but one gains the impression that respectable women covered their hair, if only casually, when they wanted to look presentable. Some fashions allowed loose hair or plaits to peep from beneath headdresses, but a fringe or curls are almost never seen.

Over the hair was worn a linen headcloth or cap, sometimes small and simple, often assuming a fashionable bulk assisted by extra layers. This was frequently covered by a second, bulkier cloth (particularly by widows and the elderly), and often worn with a veil or a long linen strip attached or pinned to the headcloth. There were many subtle variations of style, regional differences becoming more apparent towards the end of the century.

The less than perfectly smooth surfaces of the hand-made brass and iron pins used for headdresses, sleeves, etc. prevented them from falling out as easily as would modern machine-made pins.
(Photos John Howe)

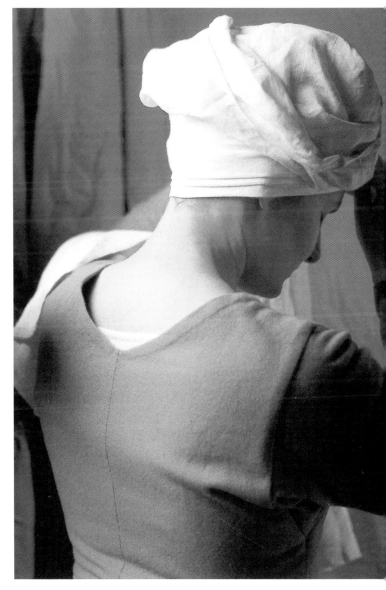

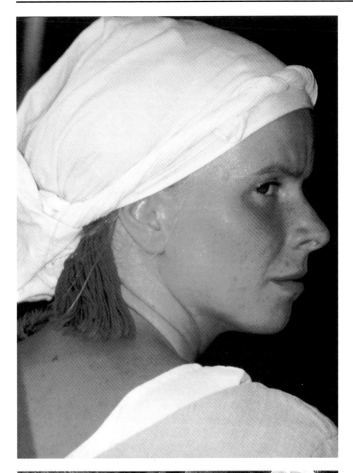

(Above left) Many of the women in the Swiss chronicles - aristocratic ladies and camp followers alike - wear coloured woollen fringes (of red, blue, green, green and red and white, or green and yellow) hanging below their headcloths in such a way as to modestly cover - or to draw attention to! - the napes of their necks. This was a fashion also to be seen in parts of Germany, but not found in any French, Italian or English illustrations. The significance, if any, of the particular colours used is not known.
(Photo Carlos Oliveira)

(Above) The fringe was mounted on a cord or headband, and worn tied round the head over encircling plaits; or tied around the head with the hair tied in two plaits at the back and looped up to the fringe-cord just in front of the ears. *(Photo Gerry Embleton)*

(Left) The women of a company of soldiers would have ample chance to supplement their normal dresses with second-hand gowns, smocks, hoods, cloaks and other clothing; on campaign they must have presented much the same appearance as their 17th and 18th century counterparts.

It is sometimes written that cloaks were seldom worn: but although it is true that garments for bad weather are not often seen in surviving late 15th century illustrations, in those that do show them cloaks both long and short occur frequently, worn by both sexes. Cloaks are not practical for working outdoors, though they are ideal for riding, marching, camp or town errands, or standing sentinel. For more active work women could wear a huke - a poncho-like garment open at the sides and perhaps belted at the waist - or an extra gown or short dress. *(Photo Gerry Embleton)*

The Masters

The rulers - the men who raised the armies and prosecuted the wars - were normally very formidable men indeed. A medieval prince or duke might be fabulously rich by modern standards: but his wealth and power had to be fought for, and defended.

He had to raise money by taxes and loans, and buy the loyalty of his subordinate noblemen, his servants and retainers. He used his family to extend his influence through marriage and to cement his grip over his realm by placing (hopefully) loyal relatives and children in positions of power. To retain his prestige and authority he had to demonstrate his wealth by dazzling display and generosity, calculating his every move to inspire admiration - and fear.

He had to know intimately the characters of his rival monarchs and of his - and their - various regional subordinates; to gauge their ambitions, strengths and weaknesses to a nicety; and to balance with exact judgement the granting or witholding of favours. It was a world little more secure for the prince than for the peasant; many great magnates lost everything to rebellion, were cut down in war, or murdered by stealthy treachery. The ruling families were to a great degree interrelated; they knew each other in peace and war - but this was far from a guarantee of solidarity. Before making any decisive move the prince had to weigh the chances of success carefully against a dozen different factors. Statecraft was a subtle, never-ending game of chess, played for the highest stakes of all. *(Photo John Howe)*

RAISING THE ARMIES

(**Above**) A powerful Savoyard lord, his trusted clerk by his side, receives a visit from a Burgundian noble on an official embassy. The Burgundian delivers a loving letter from his duke, and a loud and public demand for aid against the Bernese. The Savoyard is shocked; his reply is cautious and prevaricating. Both are trained and experienced in the game of diplomacy. Later another and more realistic conversation will take place in privacy, including the Savoyard magnate's most trusted captain. The three men – old personal friends – will discuss more freely the private policies of the Duke of Burgundy, what careful moves must be quietly made to the benefit of all, and what public gloss should be put on these decisions...*(Photo John Howe)*

(**Left**) When a medieval army set off on campaign it did not simply plunge unguided into the unknown. Merchants, pilgrims, wagoners and soldiers travelled far and frequently; many could be found who knew the countryside over which the army must pass, and others along the way who knew the roads in their own regions. There were many published travel guides for pilgrims and other regular wayfarers, and written itineraries could be consulted.

Scouts and spies would always be sent out to do their work in advance of the army. Most princes had their espionage departments; one writer even suggested that "a prince should spend a third of his revenues on spies". Bribes, gifts and promises were everyday weapons of political warfare; an agent with up-to-date knowledge of who could be influenced or "turned", and who could not, was a valuable asset. Such an agent, in turn, needed a web of informers to make himself more valuable to his employer, and thus more secure. Such spymasters might head the palace "security police", and would always know where to contact a reliable assassin should need arise. The whispers of intrigue were a constant accompaniment to court life at all levels; and during time of war loyalties could shift – could be made to shift – like smoke on the breeze. *(Photo John Howe)*

Bankers and Merchants

A powerful international banking system, far more sophisticated than we might imagine, lent the money to finance 15th century armies. Huge loans were raised - and sometimes never paid back. There was no great central bank to underpin the system, and some banks failed when client princes fell from power, or simply wrote off their debts in exasperation. It is hardly surprising that bankers operated their own espionage networks; their only real sanction against a prince's failure to repay was the refusal of future credit. In spite of the Church's ban on usury these houses operated a classic banking system, accepting deposits at interest and lending out at a higher rate.

Gold coins, because of their high value, were used for the more important transactions. Most of the coins in everyday use were minted from silver, or *billon* - silver less than fifty per cent pure - which looks almost exactly like copper.

It is very difficult to form anything like a clear picture of the actual value of medieval currencies, which were affected not only by their bullion content but also by the confidence of the market. Exchange rates fluctuated with changing monetary policies and with every shift in the political scene. At times governments fought to maintain a stable currency; at others they recklessly debased their own coinage for short term profit.

The coins of many different powers were in use throughout Europe. With abacus in one hand, and a list of exchange rates in the other (or in his cunning head), a Flemish merchant-banker of the 1490s might have to deal with the following calculations: One Burgundian cavalier = 79 Flemish groats; one St.Andrew's guilder = 61; one French franc = 68; one salut = 76; one ecu = 71; one English noble = 153; one Italian florin, genovino or ducet = 79; one Rhenish guilder = 33... One Flemish groat = one and a half Brabantine groats; 6 Artesian and Holland groats = 12 Hainault groats = 12 pence Parisis; one French pound Tournois, at 240 pence Tournois to the pound = 32 to 36 Flemish groats...

We know a lot about wages and prices from various medieval documentary sources; but comparative value - buying power - is very difficult to assess since the intrinsic value of so many everyday objects has changed out of all recognition.

Merchants used bills of exchange for very large transactions; many had branches all over Europe on which to draw funds, so as not to risk the transportation of large sums in gold. Some became rich enough to operate as bankers; these could reach dizzying heights of political influence - but only with care. The ostentatious house in Bruges of Jacques Coeur (1395-1456), dangerously like the palace of a prince, contributed to his downfall. The house of Blum in Frankfurt did over 300,000 florins' worth of business in 1491-93 alone; and Jacob Fugger became the richest man in Christendom, with perhaps two to three million florins.

There were rogues and criminals among the powerful merchant class; but many, perhaps sensitive to the Church's condemnation of certain commercial practices and to the consequent threat of Hell's fires to their immortal souls, tried to follow a balanced path, giving generously to charity and using their fortunes to benefit the community. Francisco Datini, merchant of Prato near Florence, wrote on the first page of his ledgers:"In the name of God and of profit..." *(Photo Claude Huyghens & Françoise Danrigal)*

(Overleaf) At the window of his grand house in Bruges, brand new and built in the latest style, an Italian merchant writes to his partner in Italy. Business is booming:"...now that the war is ended between the count and his cousin arms and armour may be purchased cheaply. Buy all that you can and send it south. A good price may be had, as there is trouble between the cities of..." This gentleman has recently married into a very minor branch of the Burgundian aristocracy, and intends to settle here at what seems the very heart of the financial and commercial world. With young Duke Charles's ambitions to vastly increase his well-organised army, a merchant with good contacts among the great Italian armour manufacturers (he has a Missaglia second cousin) could make a fortune...
(Photo Philippe Krauer/L'Illustré)

Recruiting

In general terms, the army of each state reflected its circumstances and culture. Mighty bureaucratic powers such as Burgundy had powerful bureaucratic armies.

By the late 15th century armies consisting of a rabble led by maverick robber-knights still existed, but were rare. It was far more effective to hire, when necessary, professional soldiers under experienced captains than to press untrained amateurs. It was unusual for an army to be under arms for very long: soldiers expected to be paid, well and regularly, and they would desert if that pay was not forthcoming. Only the richest monarchs could afford more than a sizeable permanent bodyguard; French and Burgundian attempts to create virtual standing armies were unpopular with those whose taxes paid for them.

When an army was raised it was usually well-organised, with detailed contracts between monarchs and recruiters; fixed rates of pay; rules of conduct, reward and punishment; training, and regular supply. That was, at least, the ideal; and although it often broke down, such a system was obviously necessary to any army wishing to fight a successful campaign, or even to march to its objective without starving or breaking up.

Numbers

Medieval chroniclers quoted numbers to impress rather than to convey exact figures. Hard information was difficult to come by at second hand; and even when the writer had been present in person he tended to use his imagination: "60,000 of the enemy perished" simply meant "a lot". However, account books were kept by a very different type of man: and although creative at times, they have left us muster rolls and ration lists which help us nearer to the truth. (These survive among a huge and complex range of documents which testify to an all too familiar and pettifogging bureaucracy.)

For example, the Burgundian army of Duke John the Fearless was reviewed at various times between 1405 and 1407, and actually numbered between 2,600 and 10,500 men. Contemporary chroniclers of the 1411 campaign variously reported strengths of 2,600 (at a review), 16,000, and 60,000 - needless to say, all three figures have been quoted as factual by later historians.

(Photos John Howe, Anne Embleton)

Training and Drill

The best-preserved and most detailed 15th century military instructions are the ordinances of Charles the Bold, Duke of Burgundy (r. 1467-77). He issued many: the Milanese ambassador described Charles sitting up late at night writing them. Some were copied, beautifully illuminated and bound, and handed to each captain with his baton of rank when he swore his annual allegiance to the duke. They deal with every aspect of army organisation, equipment, uniform and discipline; but the training orders in the Ordinance of St.Maximin de Trèves, October 1473, are remarkable:

"In order that the troops may be better trained and exercised in the use of arms and better practised and instructed...when they are in garrison...the captains of the squadrons and the *chambres* are from time to time to take some of their men-at-arms [armoured cavalry] out into the fields...to practise charging with the lance, keeping in close formation...to defend their ensigns, to withdraw on command, and to rally, each helping the other ...and how to withstand a charge.

"In like manner the archers with their horses, to get them used to dismounting and drawing their bows. They must learn how to attach their horses together by their bridles and make them walk forward directly behind them, attaching the horses of three archers by their bridles to the saddlebow of the page to whose man-at-arms they belong; also to march briskly forwards and to shoot without breaking rank.

"The pikemen must be made to advance in close formation in front of the said archers, kneel at a sign from them, holding their pikes lowered to the level of a horse's back so that the archers can shoot over the said pikemen as if over a wall...The archers must also learn to place themselves back to back in double defence, or in a square or a circle, always with the pikemen outside them to withstand the charge of the enemy horse, and their horses with the pages enclosed in their midst.

"The officers can begin by introducing this way of doing things to small groups and, when one of these groups is practised and instructed, they can take out others. While doing this the officers are to keep an eye on their

people every day, so that none will dare absent themselves or be without horse and armour, because they will not be sure on which day the officers will want

to take them out on exercises. Thus each will be constrained to learn to do his duty."
(Above) Burgundian halbardiers at drill. *(Photo Anne Embleton)*

(Left) A captain discusses orders with his *diseniers*. By the late 15th century the custom of issuing a set of disciplinary orders to an army seems to have been widespread, and some still survive. One military manual recommends that the rules be discussed by the commanders, and published throughout the army via officers and trumpeters "wherever there is need and in as many languages as are spoken by the men of your army". *(Photo John Howe)*

Commanders usually agreed a battle formation plan for the coming engagement, based on their knowledge of the terrain and the possible formation of the enemy. This was sometimes quite flexible, and adaptable to developments as the battle progressed. At other times the order of battle was drawn up in quite minute detail, particularly when the troops were neighbours and experienced comrades. The plan of Zurich's battle formation of 1443 survives: here one can see the men of the villages of Talwil,

(Below) Flanked by a drummer and a veteran soldier, infantry wearing the livery jacket of the dukes of Burgundy practice advancing in formation. *(Photo Hans Weber)*

Ruschlikon, Andelfingen and others each allotted to their file, next to files from the Haberdashers' Guild (ten men), the Vintners' Guild (21 men), the Blacksmiths, Boatmen and Tanners. Such exact forming-up orders would require practice, which was encouraged by law.

Charles the Bold's order of battle at Neuss on 23 May 1475 also survives. Each company had its place in the formation, drawn up in two lines, each line with its own reserves, all wearing the duke's livery and all identified by their banners.

In the 15th century the works of the Roman writer Vegetius were one of the classics frequently found in the libraries of the great, and much studied by the military. His *Regulae Bellorum Generales* was available in French and Latin, and was published in England in verse form. He wrote: "The better the troops of a garrison are trained and accustomed to discipline the less problems one will have with them during battle...Only a few men are brave by nature - good training increases their numbers". One can be sure that this self-evidently sensible advice was not ignored in 15th century armies throughout Europe, even those less minutely regulated than the troops of Charles the Bold.

Some modern historians main-

tain that the Swiss did not train: "any woodcutter who could handle an axe could handle a halbard". Perhaps - if nobody else stood within seven feet of him in any direction...but not in formation, where wild, swinging blows would split the skull of a comrade in the rank behind, and an undisciplined rush could break up the pike formation and let the enemy cavalry in.

Diagrams of manoeuvres for German troops made at the end of the 15th century show a column wheeling into line - difficult enough on a parade ground, let alone in battle. It quickly becomes obvious to anyone attempting to manoeuvre even small numbers of men carrying polearms that it is impossible to do so without some sort of instruction in weapon-handling, and a common system of drill. With close formations made up of very large numbers (e.g. a Swiss pike-and-halbard block of perhaps 1,100 men), manoeuvring under battle conditions (and such troops were certainly capable of manoeuvre), a high level of training was vital if they were to keep in the closely ordered ranks which were their *raison d'être*, and change direction without disturbing their formation. Formal ordinances or no, it was obviously in the interest of every officer and old soldier

who wished to come out of battle alive that all new recruits understood this.

Stature of recruits
In recent decades better diet and a general improvement in public health and welfare have brought about an increase in the average height of Western Europeans. The key word is average: it is wrong to imagine that "everyone was smaller in those days", and the entire population has not become steadily taller in a continuous progression over the ages. Six-foot-tall Neolithic skeletons have been found; there were six-foot archers at Agincourt; and there are short men in today's armies. Average heights from large samples of 14th century battle-grave skeletons, British infantrymen of 1815, and British First World War recruits are all the same - 5ft.6ins. tall; but each sample includes many men taller than the average. Regional and class differences in physique were probably wider at all times before the mid-20th century. Several chroniclers of the day comment on the size of the English archers; and Henry VIII's Yeomen of the Guard in the early 16th century were described as giants. The author has handled medieval armour to fit any size of modern man.

(Left) A cloaked officer watches a small body of infantry training with polearms.
(Photo Hans Weber)

(Left) The Swiss chronicler Schilling decribed troops from Entlebuch and Lucerne taking part in the "armour show" on the Zinstag during Lucerne's autumn fair. They made a brave enough show, mostly pikemen behind their drummers; but:

"It was at that time a praiseworthy old custom, for the good of the city of Lucerne, that all citizens would come together on the great Zinstag during the autumn fair [in 1478 this fell on 6 October] and, after the evening meal, put on their armour and practice the use of weapons. This happened at night, so perhaps much went undone that should have been done, and it would have been better to prevent this. But arrogance caused things to be left as they were. At that time it was the law that the use of armour be practised, and the old people paid more attention to this than people do now."

Imminent danger encouraged efficiency, but in more relaxed times "muster days" in towns and cities across Europe must have been more of a celebration than anything else - reminiscent of later militia musters.
(Photo Anik Diserans)

THE OFFICERS

Below the prince, duke, bishop, city council, or their designated commander served a range of officers: knights, men-at-arms, and professional mercenary captains who led the troops in the field. There were no fixed ranks as in later armies, and a "captain" might command anything from a small band to an army. They might be inexperienced but high-born youths, ambitious politicians, ruthless brigands, professional soldiers, or a potentially explosive mixture of all these.

Among them were many experienced men. seriously interested in their craft and accustomed to its hardships.

War, politics, building, painting and writing were already thought of as scientific activities; the ways of the Ancients were thought superior, to be studied with care - Machiavelli wrote that "the ancestors did all things better and with greater prudence than us". In the military libraries of monarchs and notables were translations of treatises on military theory, practice, engineering and science, copied and recopied until the age of printing allowed them to circulate widely at lower levels.

In a "modern" 15th century army a good officer had to master paperwork, organisation,

tactics - and his often unruly men, setting an example in civil life and in battle. Some shone as courtiers, rising from humble backgrounds to exalted rank. But officers led their armies from the front, and only the fit, strong, clever and lucky survived. Fitness came from lifelong riding, hunting and martial activities. The ideal was a strong, active man to whom growing experience and maturity would bring good judgement. Many, of course, fell short of this ideal: the uncontrollable whims of hot-headed young aristocrats, proud, jealous, and deaf to advice, often brought careful plans to ruin.
(Photo Gerry Embleton)

(Left) An officer of the Duke of Warwick's household in the 1470s. This well-dressed gentleman wears a barbute helmet, which recalls the classical lines of an ancient Greek model. Its narrow face opening gives a surprisingly good field of vision and good ventilation while affording excellent protection. Italian styles were widely copied elsewhere, though this helmet could have been purchased from Italy - or the gentleman might even be an Italian soldier himself: all Christendom was the professional soldier's field to plough. His livery is Warwick's red and white, and bears his badge: an embroidered silver "bear and ragged staff" with gold chain and collar. Many of Warwick's household wore simple badges of the ragged staff alone. *(Photo John Howe)*

(Above) From *The Art of War* by Taccola, a 15th century Italian engineer:
"The Captain must, if possible, establish his army's camp on high ground, and so be in such a position to see if his enemy is in order or disarray. He may then attack when he chooses, when his enemy is eating or sleeping at noon, or when the heat has obliged them to lay down their arms.... The place chosen for the camp must be protected by a body of water or a river, with ample water for cooking and horses, and that this place have trees on it. If there is no natural protection a ditch must be dug in front of the camp.... There must be bread and water (wine for the worthiest) in sufficient quantity. The army must have ample provisions of beef or meat powder.... The army must also have in reserve for the troops a herd of sheep or cattle...."
(Photo Philippe Krauer/ L'Illustré)

(Above right) "...If the Captain must go anywhere - by night or by day - he must do so fully armed, accompanied by crosbowmen with steel crossbows at the ready, and great ferocious hounds trained to protect his person.... When the

Captain is in enemy or hostile territory he must know the populations, their modes of government, and the riches of the enemies in question. He must know who his enemies count as friends and allies, whether they live in mountainous terrain or in the valleys, or on the plain near the sea, a lake, swamps or rivers. If he does not know all this by personal experience he must nonetheless be familiar with the provinces, countries, cities, strongholds, castles and other places, so that he never be at the mercy of a guide. When he has mastered all this, he may look to details, and by his prudence and knowledge the palm of victory will be his...."
(Photo John Howe)

(Right) "...A Captain must be wise, by nature circumspect, master of his emotions, audacious, ever vigilant, well versed in the sciences, scrupulous, true to his word, accustomed to war, a doughty fighter, and be able to hold his tongue. These are the essential qualities...without them he is like a ship without rudder or sails...."
(Photo Gerry Embleton)

(**Opposite & left**) This Imperial officer, with his escort of halbardiers, wears a short gown - a fashionable civilian garment - over his brigandine and mail. He has slung his hat - a *chaperon* - over his right shoulder supported by its hanging tail tucked into his belt. His dagger - a *Degen* in the Swiss style, approaching the proportions of a shortsword - hangs from the front of his belt, and a simple hand-and-a-half sword from his left hip. A visored sallet and bevor completely protect his head, face and throat. This is the sort of costume that might be worn by an officer in any European army from the 1450s to the end of the century.

The rear view shows the sweep of the tail of his deep German sallet. protecting the nape; the *chaperon* hanging over his shoulder; and, on the face of his sword scabbard, small sheaths for an eating knife and an awl. *(Photos John Howe)*

(**Right**) Condottiere: an Italian mercenary captain, arrayed for war in a fine Milanese armour. *(Photo Gerry Embleton)*

ARMOUR

Armour production

The image of the lonely blacksmith hammering out a single helmet in his little country forge is far from reality. Important producers such as the Missaglia family of Milan employed whole villages, mass-producing armour for sale Europe-wide. A single community might specialise in mail: some drawing wire, some fashioning the mail rings, and master craftsmen tailoring the finished mail garments. Water-powered hammers and huge grinding wheels speeded production of plate armour. Packed in straw-filled barrels, Italian armour was shipped all over the continent.

The same was happening in the great armour-producing centres of southern Germany such as Augsburg. Each manufacturing city studied the others' styles, and copied them in whole or in part when they seemed to offer improvements. Italian and German armourers laboured alongside native French, Burgundian and English craftsmen in their own countries. Although armour was produced in every country, two styles remained dominant, with adaptations to suit local tastes: "German", with its spiky outline and fluted surfaces, and the more smooth and rounded "Italian".

Armour was produced to suit every pocket. A lord would order an armour made to his exact measurements and decorated in his preferred taste; "ammunition" armour for the common soldiers was mass-produced, bought second-hand, captured, and refurbished. Old armours were frequently adapted to new fashions; hopelesly out of date armours were cut up to make brigandine plates, and finally sold for scrap metal to be forged again. Helmets no longer `a la mode` were re-formed: an old bascinet could make a new kettle hat. We have examples of 15th century visored sallet skulls being turned into "archers" visorless sallets, or being fitted with neck and cheek guards to serve as a cavalry trooper's helmet 200 years later.

A few examples suffice to give an idea of the scale of armour and weapons production and purchase:

As early as 1295 representatives of Philip the Fair bought at Bruges 2,853 helmets; 4,511 padded jacks; 751 pairs of gauntlets; 6,309 shields; 1,885 crossbows and 666,258 crossbow quarrels; 14,599 swords and daggers; 13,495 lance and spear heads....Cicca Simonetta promised the Duke of Milan that three armourers and their assistants contracted to him could make enough equipment for six men-at-arms every day.

Countless lists survive of military equipment contracted for by armourers and merchants: 100 armours a year for Charles the Bold; 50 complete suits in the Burgundian fashion each year for three years for Maximilian von Hapsburg. The quantity and the speed of production should come as no surprise; how else could the armies have been equipped?

(Photos: below, Claude Huyghens & Françoise Danrigal; bottom, John Howe)

The Knight

The knight was a mounted warrior who, in return for his lord's protection and provision, gave military service. By the end of the 12th century his position in most European societies was much like the familiar romantic picture. Ideas of chivalric behaviour (largely reserved for his social equals, male and female), of ceremonious investiture and ritualised training- the joust - had developed alongside a vast body of literature and song praising the knightly ideal. While this was sometimes taken to absurd lengths by a few would-be saintly individuals, it generally formed a fairly thin civilising veneer over tough, wilful and often cruel professional fighting men.

Knighthood was usually con- ferred by a ruling prince, entailing previous service as a page and years of intensive training. The title, and the property which went with it - whose revenues financed the knight's ability to give military service when called - could be passed down to the eldest son. The rights of property were the foun- dation of all wealth; and as the centuries rolled by the family tree, with its symbolic heraldic embellishments, became increasingly important as the pedigree confirming those rights - and the thicket of intermarriage, often across national borders, which underpinned them. As in every other class, however, there was constant social mobility in both directions. Some knights became immensely rich; others descended into penury. For the landless knight the only possible life was that of the hired soldier.

By the 15th century knights formed the broad foundation of the ruling class. They were proud, violent and ambitious. Some chose to serve God against the infidel, fighting under the banners of the great military-religious Orders; most followed the pursuit of power, wealth and pleasure. The tournament gave them the opportunity to show off their individual prowess, and war tested it. Wrote Roger de Hoveden: "A knight cannot distinguish himself in that if he has not trained for it in tourneys. He must have seen his blood flow, heard his teeth crack under fist blows, felt his opponent's weight bear down upon him as he lay on the ground and, after being twenty times unhorsed, have risen twenty times to fight."

As a class they usually had more in common with enemies of the same rank than with the common people of their own lands.
(Photo Ian Ashdown)

Weight and Mobility

There is no doubt that a fit man in well-fitting armour could run, jump into the saddle, and climb a ladder. Contemporary accounts and modern experiments prove this to be so - and how else could the knight and man-at-arms have fought and survived in battle? Hollywood, confused by the surviving super-heavy, less articulated armours worn solely for the joust, has created a completely false impression of knights before battle being lifted into the saddle by cranes, and lying helpless as turned turtles when knocked to the ground. The distinction between tournament armour and war armour is absolute. In the latter the plates are attached to the body, and the weight distributed, in a balanced way, allowing a man accustomed to it by long training sufficient agility to fight hand-to-hand.

There exists a 15th century illustration of a knight turning a handstand or cartwheel in full armour - a feat duplicated with ease in the photograph **(above)**. Froissart mentions Sir John Assueton leaping fully armed onto his warhorse; and Olivier de la March describes Galliot de Balthasin leaping fully armed out of the saddle "as though he had on a pourpoint only" in 1446. The chronicler Schilling even recorded that "a man-at-arms in full armour was thrown off the bridge into the Moselle. This same man called on St.Nicolas for

aid, and with the help of the saint managed to climb out of the river and survive."

From the author's own experience, the knight's main problems were ventilation and close range visibility. A closed helmet quickly becomes hot and stuffy; and although some designs give surprisingly good vision, others restrict it dangerously. It is no surprise that we read of the preference for open helmets, or of knights leaving aside their bevors - throat and lower face plates - despite the increased risk and sometimes fatal consequences. A knight who retained full protection, fighting with a lowered visor, might often fall relatively easy prey to two or three much less well equipped assailants who came at him from different angles.

Some comparative weights may be instructive. Four typical late 15th century armours average 52lbs. total weight. Examples of individual parts are: armet (close helmet), 6lbs.-7lbs.8oz.; gorget, 9oz.; two-part breastplate, 12lbs. 8oz.; tassets, 1 lb. 11oz.; right arm, 2lbs.14oz.; left arm, 2lbs. 9oz.; legs, 6lbs. 1oz. each; mailshirts with short and long sleeves, 15lbs.7oz. and 20lbs. 11 oz.; a typical sword, 2lbs.8oz.

An infantry soldier in everyday marching equipment, from the Napoleonic period to the present day, has typically carried between 60 and 70lbs., much less evenly distributed than the weight of an armour. *(Photo Gerry Embleton)*

Arming doublets

"Arming doublet" was a term used, confusingly, to describe not only what was worn under armour, to pad the body, but also sometimes what was worn over it, embroidered with the wearer's arms.

(Above & above right)

Under an armour one needs a strong jacket, without wrinkles, reinforced along the seams and lightly padded where the plates rub. Most well-made armour fits well and close to the body; the arming doublet was a foundation garment to support the plates which were, in some cases, tied directly to it by means of "points" passing from the doublet through holes in the plates. Vulnerable areas such as the armpit and inner elbow might also be protected by sections of mail attached to the doublet. The arming doublet became acceptable "off duty" attire for nobles and soldiers alike, and also influenced civilian styles. They seem frequently to have been red or grey, made of strong linen fabric.

Though illustrations are extremely rare, we have two good descriptions of what should ideally be worn under armour. A 15th century document describes how a man should be armed for the joust when fighting on foot:

"He shall have no shirt upon him, but a doublet of fustian lined with satin, cut full of

holes. The doublet must be strongly bound where the points are set about the great [part] of the arm, and the best before and behind, and the gussets of mail must be sewed to the doublet at the bend of the arm and under the arm. The arming points must be made of fine twine such as men used to make strings for crossbows, and they must be tied small and pointed as points. They must be waxed with shoe-maker's wax, and then they will neither stretch nor break.

"He shall have a pair of hose of worsted cloth, and a pair of short pads of thin blanket to put about his knees to prevent chafing of his leg harness; also a pair of shoes of thick leather, and they must be fastened with small whipcord, three knots upon a cord, and three cords must be fast sewed to the heel of the shoe, and fine cords in the middle of the sole of the same shoe...."

A Spanish painting of the period shows hose finely quilted vertically, like corduroy, without toes or heels; and another document describes: "...A pair of hose of cord without vamps [without the part covering the front of the foot] and the said hose cut at the knees and lined with linen cloth on the bias as the hose is. A pair of shoes of red leather thin laced and fretted underneath with whipcord. The shoes should be lined

from toe to above the ankle with linen cloth three fingers wide, doubled and cut on the bias, and also behind from the sole half a quarter of a yard up this to fasten well to his sabetons." *(Photos John Howe)*

Arming the knight

With the help of his squire, a knight or man-at-arm's full armour was put on in the following manner.

Gussets of mail were tied onto his arming doublet and hose with strong waxed cord, and the surplus cord cut off. A collar of mail was put on, buckled or buttoned at the side or rear; and tight mail "shorts" over the hose, also fastened with points.

The first pieces of armour put on were the metal plate shoes or *sabetons;* then the *greaves,* enclosing the calf of the leg and hinged vertically down the outside.

The *cuisse* (thigh piece) and *poleyn* (knee piece) followed, strapped against the leg and probably held to the top of the

hose at the thigh with a lace. Breast and back plates, with attached skirt piece or *fauld,* came next, and were buckled down the right side. The arm and shoulder pieces were laced to the arming doublet at the shoulder and buckled about the arms in four major parts: the *pauldron* protecting the shoulder, the *rarebrace* on the upper arm, the *couter* at the elbow, and the *vambrace* on the forearm. Spurs, helmet, sword and dagger would complete his equipment. Various coats bearing the wearer's arms or his lord's livery were worn in combat - absolutely vital identification in battle.

Most fully armoured men-at-arms fought on foot with poll-axes ("poll" meaning head), combinations of axe, hammer and spike standing about man-high and often with a rondel to protect the hand about half way up the shaft. This was an extremely effective weapon capable of delivering terrible crushing, cutting and puncturing blows.

This is a composite armour typical of the elegant Italian style of c.1450; parts of it bear Milanese marks. The helmet, one of the most popular types, is an armet; in the rear view note the large disc plate fixed to the back of it, probably to protect the straps of the reinforce plate attached to the lower front of the helmet, and to stop them sliding. Note the heavily armoured left shoulder and arm - the side presented to the enemy - and the smaller right shoulder plate cut away so that the lance can be couched in the lance rest. The rest might be hinged so that it could be folded out of the way, or fastened in place when needed with a peg. *(Private collection; photos Ian Ashdown)*

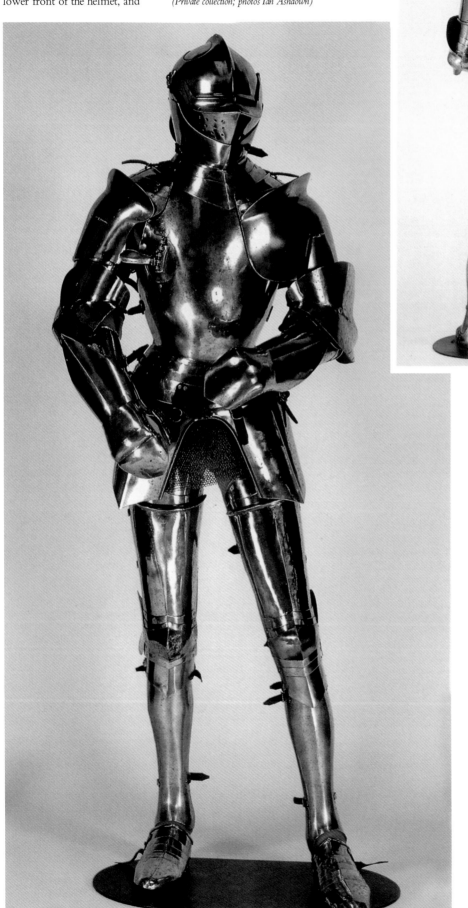

A composite armour made in the style of Jörg Treytz of Innsbruck and typically Tyrolean in form - slightly smoother in outline than the products of more northerly centres.

Men-at-arms of all nations would have worn armours like these; those of princes and dukes would have been breathtakingly ornamented, perhaps totally gilded, polished like mirrors and blazing in the sunlight.
(Private collection; photos Ian Ashdown)

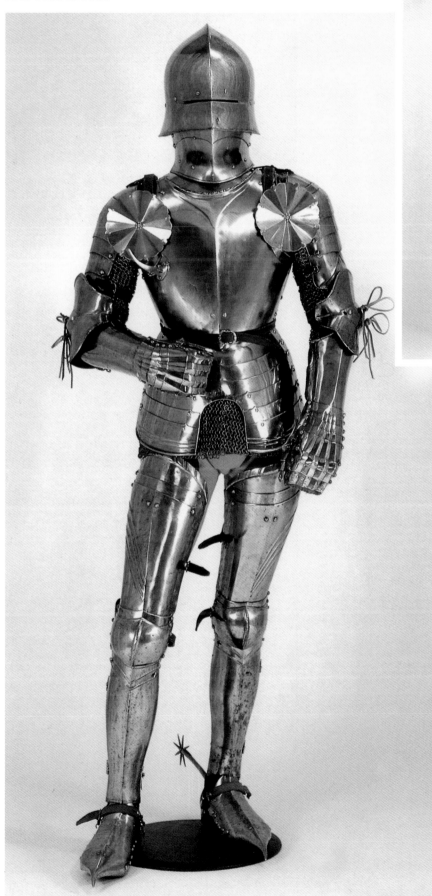

(Below, and side view opposite) This - like most other 15th century armours surviving today - is a composite: composed of separate pieces originally made for different armours. Even in the 15th century some composites were probably worn, as expensive armours were adapted to changes in the owner's physique, or suits were made up from captured or second-hand parts. This Italian armour is made in the style associated with Lombardy, c.1470, evidently for a more solidly built man than the wasp-waisted example on page 36. The armet has an attached mail collar and a large eyeslit, and seems to have been made without a visor. *(Private collection; photos Ian Ashdown)*

(Above) The same armour brought to life, worn by a living man, and here with a deep barbute rather than an armet. This shows the elegant overlapping "wings" of the shoulder plates. *(Photo Gerry Embleton)*

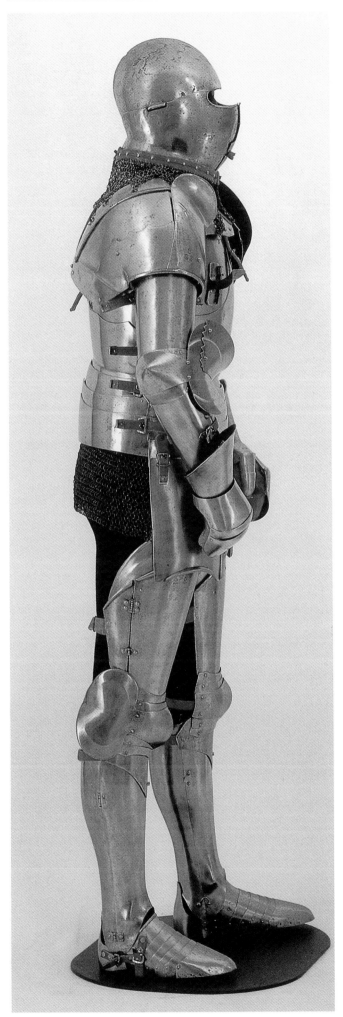

(Below) Rear view of a fine German man-at-arms' armour, with heavily fluted surfaces, worn with a deep sallet whose tail protects the top of the spine. Note the back plate of three overlapping pieces and the skirt of lames, which give great flexibility.

Even good reconstructions can scarcely do justice to the marvellous craftsmanship of original 15th century armours. The thickness of each hammered-out plate varies depending on its function - thickest where it might receive a blow, thinnest where it is protected or where it passes under another plate. Close-fitting, the moving parts pass over each other without leaving a gap that a fine blade might enter; in movement there is none of the "clank and rattle" that often characterises modern reconstructions.

A first class armour was expensive, aesthetically pleasing and wonderfully functional. Even "ammunition" armour was rarely crude, often showing a high level of craftsmanship and that natural eye for form that was, until recently, an essential part of the handwork carried out at every level of society.
(Photo Gerry Embleton)

Horse armour

(Left) The knight in all his splendour, armoured for war. This horse armour was probably made for Waldemar VI of Anhalt-Zerbst (1450-1508); the knight's composite armour is of the same period, the sallet bearing the armourer's mark of Jörg Treytz of Innsbruck. *(Photo courtesy the Board of Trustees of the Royal Armouries)*

Although it is sometimes found listed as part of the regulation equipment of a man-at-arms, horse armour - weighing perhaps 60 to 70lbs., and a bulky piece of equipment - was not frequently worn on campaign. It is rarely mentioned in English household accounts; contemporary illustrations such as those in the Swiss chronicles, Italian battle paintings and various manuscripts show many, if not a majority, of unarmoured horses in battle. Some, however, wear a metal chamfron to protect their vulnerable heads.

Many men-at-arms also preferred to lighten their own armour, wearing open helmets such as sallets and kettle hats, brigandines or breast plates, arm protection, and perhaps cuisses with long boots. A fully armoured knight and horse could certainly gallop and charge, but could not keep going all day long without frequent rests. It seems probable that full armour was put on only on occasions when a severe engagement was expected, when ample transport was available and there was plenty of time to prepare for battle beforehand.

Horses

We do not know a great deal about medieval horses; certainly, there were many local breeds unrecorded and long since forgotten. It was an equestrian age, and hunting and various types of mounted tournament were the consuming passions of the aristocracy. The usual riding seat was much the same as that of the American West - with long stirrups, so that the rider almost stood in a saddle which was constructed to give support before and behind. This was very comfortable for a day in the saddle, and gave a secure seat for striking blows with sword or lance.

Horses obviously played a major part in medieval warfare. They were used as draught and pack animals; and not only the men-at-arms but also many archers and crossbowmen were mounted, dismounting to fight like latter-day dragoons. A description of 1465 states that the Burgundian army were mostly horsemen, "except for those who brought up the guns", and certain classes of footsoldiers such as pikemen. The men-at-arms usually dismounted to fight with the archers, "in order that the common soldiers might be reassured and fight better"; wrote Philippe de Commynes, "they had learnt this method from the English...."

The cavalry of the 15th century would have operated at much the same speeds as their descendants of the Napoleonic age or the Great War. Roads and terrain affected their performance, as did the supply of feed and water, and the weather; but the final limits were set by the animal itself.

In the 19th century the British Army laid down that large bodies of cavalry could normally cover 20-25 miles per day at a steady walk. Sometimes trotting, they might make a forced march of 40-45 miles; or even double this, if they ignored the inevitable damage to the horses. Smaller formations of several hundred might manage 30 miles in a day, with more time to rest.

Horses are not machines; they can be difficult, and take a great deal of management on campaign. It can take all night to water a thousand horses at a small stream in the dark; imagine the difficulties of a medieval army with 10,000 horses to water and feed, moving through sparsely populated hills in February... Armies with thousands of horses cannot have relied solely on foraging along the way, and large numbers of feed wagons must have accompanied the tail of the march. It is generally held that a horse can carry about a quarter of its own weight; an average early 20th century cavalry mount weighed around 1,000lbs., giving a useful load of 250lbs. - under campaign conditions British cavalry carried just over 280lbs. The value of such comparisons is severely limited by our ignorance of medieval horses; but for what it is worth, an armour, helmet and sword weighed about 60lbs., a rider and saddle perhaps 170lbs. for a total of 230lbs., and horse armour an additional 70lbs.

(Above right) Archers in the service of the Count of Thierstein in Alsace take their horses to the village smith. They are on guard- these are troubled times, and they are at war with Burgundy.

Because of the growth of the hoof a horseshoe is supposed to last only about a month. Late 19th century army horseshoes, not much different from medieval ones, were reckoned to wear out after 150-250 miles of road work. The presence of skilled men and specialised tools was essential for a horse army, although many more people than today would have been "horse wise". Forges would have been available along the populated routes, but smiths must have accompanied the baggage train of any well-organised army. *(Photos Suzanne Hupfer)*

The late 15th century English archer often rode to battle; and could - contrary to modern misconceptions - shoot from horseback, although they were obviously vastly more effective when they dismounted to fight. These archers, wearing helmets and thick jacks, have dismounted to scout; their bows are still in the bags which protected them from damp on the march. The long boots are typical of horsemen of all ranks. *(Photo Gerry Embleton)*

Helmets

Helmets were the most commonly worn piece of armour, and hundreds of thousands were in use throughout Europe. Those surviving in our museums must be seen in the context of contemporary illustrations, manuscripts and paintings. There were countless different shapes; examples of only a few of these - and not always the most commonly worn - have survived by random chance. (There were also headpieces of leather, wickerwork, etc., but we have little direct evidence of their forms.) Later historians have tried to categorise the survivors into a rigid typology; but in their written accounts 15th century clerks might use the term "sallet" for anything from a small skullcap to a deep helmet protecting cheeks and neck which would today be described as a "barbute".

So-called kettle hats of many differing shapes were commonly worn. The classic broad-brimmed form, supposedly the inspiration for the British shrapnel helmet of the Great War, is familiar; but simple deep bowls not too unlike the 1940s US M1 appear in Swiss chronicles; bell-shaped helmets, sometimes with eyeslits in the brim, were seen in northern Europe; more decorative forms with pointed or fluted skulls, not unlike some 16th century helmets, seem to have been worn in France and Burgundy; and all these variations travelled and intermingled.

The barbute was very popular in Italy, some with a T-shaped face slit resembling an ancient Greek form. The very varied shapes of sallet - from the simplest nut-shaped skull, to deep, sweeping, visored forms drawn out in a long rear tail - were ubiquitous. A feature which does not survive on any extant helmets but which is fairly common in illustrations is a short hanging neckguard of overlapping plates attached to the rear.

All helmets had a padded lining, and were held firmly to the head by stout buckled chinstraps, tied thongs, or a single broad strap buckled to the back plate at the base of the neck. Helmets were brilliantly polished, left black from the forge, gilded, painted, or covered in cloth. Some were richly decorated with gilded ornaments and precious stones. Ostrich and other plumes were used in profusion.

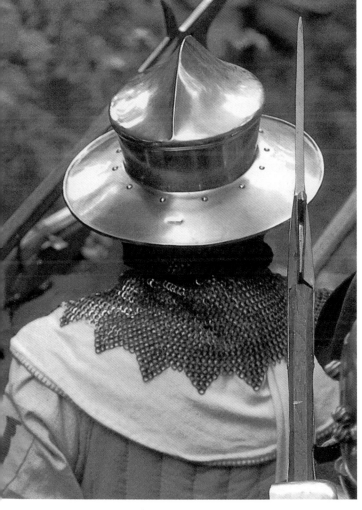

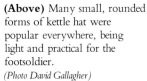

(**Above**) Many small, rounded forms of kettle hat were popular everywhere, being light and practical for the footsoldier.
(Photo David Gallagher)

(**Left**) Deep kettle hat of a form favoured in Germany and Bohemia, but also seen elsewhere. *(Photo John Howe)*

(**Top**) Kettle hat of a deep, curved form popular in France and Burgundy, but made in northern Italy c. 1480.
(Photo Gerry Embleton)

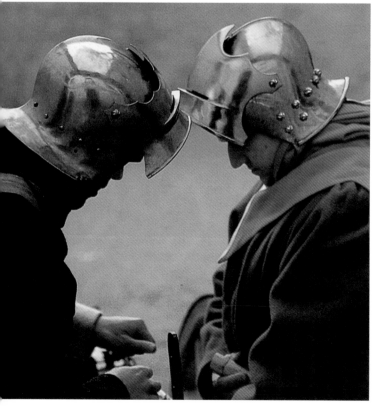

(Opposite top) A very deep visored sallet of German style. *(Photo Carlos Oliveira)*

(Above left & above) This visored sallet, left black from the forge as a protection against rust, is worn with the visor slightly lifted. This is often depicted in manuscript illustrations; the soldier can see, but is protected against missiles. *(Photos Alan & Michael Perry)*

(Opposite bottom left) Two artillerymen wearing visored sallets with the visors up. This general form seems to have been the most popular single type of helmet throughout 15th century Europe. *(Photo John Howe)*

(Centre & left) Two views of a deep visored sallet; note the rivets to secure the padded lining and chinstrap, both essential features but missing from surviving helmets. *(Photos David Gallagher)*

(Left) A visored sallet with a pointed skull, as made in England but in the French fashion. *(Photo Alan & Michael Perry)*

(Right, top & bottom) Helmets of every conceivable form, from skull to barbute, were commonly worn throughout the continent, varying in workmanship from superb to extremely simple. *(Photos John Howe)*

(Below left) The simplest soldier's sallet - nearly a bowl-shaped skullcap. *(Photo Alan & Michael Perry)*

(Below) A richly ornamented light sallet, suitable for this archer of the retinue of Richard of Gloucester, later Richard III of England; he wears his master's boar badge on his coat in livery colours. We know that many helmets were ornamented, but surviving examples are rare. *(Photo Gerry Embleton)*

Brigandines

(Below) Lighter and more flexible than plate, brigandines were popular among all classes of fighting men, and were even convenient enough to be worn by travellers in dangerous country. They figure in lists and accounts all over Europe; their manufacture was controlled for quality, and many were "proved" by having a crossbow bolt shot at them. Small overlapping armour plates, tinned against rust, were rivetted to a canvas waistcoat and usually covered with a better material; the visible rivet heads were tinned, silvered, gilded, or stamped with simple designs. Sometimes two large plates protected the chest; sometimes brigandine-work short sleeves and tassets were added.

It is clear that body defences using many combinations of fabric and plate, of metal, horn, leather and mail were in simultaneous use; but we only fully understand the jack and the brigandine. *(Photo John Howe)*

Jacks

(Left & above) Fabric armour - padded, stuffed or many-layered, sometimes interlined with plates of metal or horn - was widely worn. Historians have tried to categorise subtle differences between terms - jacks, jazerines, pourpoints, brigandines, etc. - which were used more loosely by contemporary writers. The jack, made of many layers of quilted cloth (up to 30) or stuffed with rags, was worn by many infantrymen and archers. In 1483 soldiers of the Duke of Gloucester are described wearing "comfortable tunics... stuffed with tow...They say that the softer the tunics the better do they withstand the blows of arrows and swords, and besides that in summer they are lighter and in winter more serviceable than iron". A detailed specification from the ordinances of Louis XI of France for the construction of jacks with 25 or 30 cloth layers and one of "stag's skin" claims that "never have been seen half a dozen men killed by stabs or arrow wounds in such jacks...". In 1467 Charles VII of France ordered the brigandines of his *franc archiers* replaced by jacks. The jack and sallet seem to have been the typical gear of the well-equipped footsoldier; the combination appeal's not only in clerks' lists, but in contexts where it is used as symbolic shorthand for the fighting man: "In every shire with jakkes and salades clean misrule doth rise", wrote John Hardyng during the Wan of the Roses. *(Photos Gerry Embleton)*

WEAPONS

Footsoldiers

By the middle of the 15th century there was a general move to recruit more infantry. Formerly the battle potential of all except specialist footsoldiers such as archers and crossbowmen had often been neglected. The new trend was partly for economic reasons - "general purpose" infantry were cheaper; but also because commanders began to understand their value if well organised and disciplined. Everything hinged on their ability to move in cohesive formations, and to stand against attack; their value lay in their mass - once broken, they were a rabble.

Achievement lagged behind ambition. Both Louis XI of France and Charles the Bold of Burgundy, among other commanders, tried to train up disciplined units of foot with varying success; but they could never keep sufficient numbers in the field for long enough, or find a unifying factor that would hold them together through thick and thin. That would take long service, strict discipline, and money.

The increasing popularity of the pike - a useless weapon in anything but an unbroken massed formation - encouraged an understanding among the soldiers of the vital importance of standing shoulder to shoulder and moving as one. The Swiss had an early advantage in this respect; their men were lined up in files according to their village or guild, each conscious of being under the eyes of his neighbours and accustomed comrades. By the end of the century an Italian observer could say of them that they "drilled like a machine". It was the Swiss, too, in their wars against Burgundy, who demonstrated the tactical possibilities of integrated formations of pikemen, halbardiers, swordsmen and missile infantry - crossbowmen and handgunners.

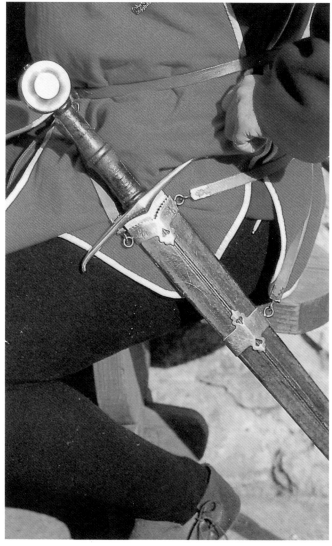

(Above) Although quality naturally varied with wealth, some kind of sword was carried as the personal sidearm by most soldiers of every rank, and was the final arbiter of hand-to-hand combat.
(Photo Philippe Krauer/ L'Illustr'e)

(Right) A classic form of the knight's or well-paid professional soldier's sword.
(Photo Gerry Embleton)

The sword was *the* knightly weapon - symbolic of the fighting man's status and dignity; perhaps at least in part an heirloom from his fathers; and in battle, literally "his life in his hands". The ponderous, shield-hacking cleaver of Hollywood melodrama bears no relation to the truth; the real thing was surprisingly light for its size, a perfectly balanced precision tool - the very best that money could buy. Many rich men owned several swords in different styles: single-hand swords for cutting and general purpose work; long, stiff thrusting swords; weapons of particularly beautiful workmanship for ceremonial and the display of their taste and wealth. No doubt they each had their favourite, the perfect battle weapon which balanced in the hand like an extension of the body and will.

All the techniques of swordfighting illustrated in the surviving manuscripts are sophisticated and, as modern experiments have shown, both practical and deadly. Men practised in these techniques with large 15th century swords display all the speed and agility of modern fencers or students of Kendo. Fighting for your life against a fit, highly trained swordsman was a very serious business indeed.

(Photos Gerry Embleton)

Especially popular in the second half of the 15th century was the "bastard" or "hand-and-a-half" sword, with its long, well-balanced hilt. A special school of fencing had grown up in Italy and Germany devoted to this weapon for "combats of justice" and other fighting techniques. The Guild of St. Marcus and the Holy Virgin was formed in Frankfurt; its pupils, mostly former craftsmen and students, became fencing masters, and gradually spread their knowledge throughout Europe.

In the late 14th century one Master Liechtenaur published in manuscript a great work on fencing; but it was his pupil, Master Thalhoffer - four of whose books survive - who became the most famous of the German sword-masters. Thalhoffer and his colleagues drew upon each other's published works shamelessly; the fencing books were copied and recopied, and with the spread of printing in the latter half of the 15th century many more fencing masters rushed to publication.

The sword-masters were hired by the aristocracy; in 1485 Thalhoffer instructed the Duke of Württemberg in preparation for his pilgrimage to the Holy Land. They also set up schools in what would now be called gymnasia or health centres - and in the marketplace. They instructed town guildsmen, and the young toughs whose swaggering image - with long hair, very tight, slit doublet, and long sword - figures in many chronicles and prints of the time.

There is evidence for the spread of their influence to France and Britain, and although there was occasional legislation against these foreign swordsmen they seem to have prospered in spite of it. *(Photos Gerry Embleton)*

(Right) The hilts of two typical 15th century "hand-and-a-half" swords and a single-hand sword, with the type of small knife and awl sometimes seen sheathed on the face of sword scabbards. *(Photo Gerry Embleton)*

Sword and Buckler

Fighting with sword and buckler, using both as offensive and defensive weapons, was a highly developed technique; a south German fencing manual of c. 1300 shows much the same moves as books ot the late 15th century.

Many common soldiers carried bucklers - small iron fist-shields, of either convex or concave shape - dangling from the hilts of their sheathed swords; and the swaggering bully, "sword and buckler by his side", figures in many ballads and illustrations. One gains the impression that, in England at least, they could be as essential a badge of masculine credibility as the holstered revolver of the Old West. At various times during the 15th century the authorities either encouraged sword-and-buckler play as a useful training for potential soldiers; or banned it as a threat to the king's peace, unacceptably costly in lives and limbs.

(Left & above) Usually a short sword or curved falchion was held in the right hand and the buckler in the left. Arms outstretched, the swordsman laid his blade across his buckler, effectively blocking his opponent's blows with the strength of both arms. The boss of the buckler (sometimes pointed) and its rim were used to strike boxing blows, unbalancing the opponent and creating opportunities for cuts with the sword. *(Photos John Howe)*

The common soldiery favoured swords of a variety of shapes: simple cut-and-thrust swords with straight blades and cross quillons; heavy single-edged falchions, with a variety of curved blades reminiscent of broad "scimitars" and later infantry hangers; and various special forms such as Austrian and German hunting swords. The basilard-hilted Swiss *Degen* **(right)**, popular beyond the Confederation's borders throughout the second half of the century, varied in length from a dagger to a short sword; this was the ancestor of the so-called "Holbein" daggers. **(Far right)** A simple soldier's sword with recurved quillons, an eating knife and an awl or steel sheathed on the scabbard; such weapons were traded all over Europe.
(Photos Gerry Embleton & John Howe)

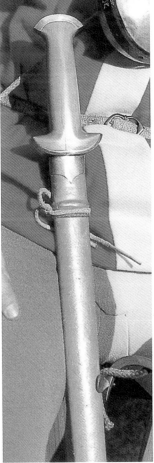

Polearms

Many different forms of polearms - long-shafted weapons - were used by the 15th century footsoldier. Some evolved from farm implements, like the flail, scythe, fork, axe and bill; some from weapons of the hunt, like the boar spear; and some were developed for the special needs of the battlefield - the halbard in its many variations, and the pike. In the 15th century there were almost as many variations as there were smiths to forge them; later historians' attempts to impose rigid classifications under one or other of the contemporary terms would not have been recognised by the original owners.

Pikes are primarily defensive, charge-stopping weapons: no horse will impale itself on a hedge of steel points, and few men are suicidally brave or foolhardy enough to do so. Supported by missile weapons, footsoldiers armed with halbard, bill or sword sought to hack an exploitable gap in each others' formations. Doubtless the opposing forces often slowed their advance as they neared one another, finally stopping at spear's length, jabbing and cutting but hesitating to be the first to push forward into the enemy's whirling thicket of steel points and cutting edges. The first to do so must have been a brave man indeed - perhaps leaping into a momentary gap cut by arrow or shot, or over shafts forced down by the weight of an unlucky comrade's corpse...

(Right) A well-armed English billman of Edward IV's household stands sentinel. He wears visored sallet, mail "standard" or collar, breast plate, and stout jack with laced-on sleeves. His livery jacket in blue and murray bears one of the royal badges, the white rose of York. Plate armour protects his vulnerable thighs and knees, but his shins and feet are left free for mobility. His hooked bill, one of many forms developed from an agricultural implement common throughout Europe, was a great favourite of the English. "Billmen" was a term used to describe footsoldiers armed with a wide variety of polearms, just as "spearmen" covered a variety of spears and pikes.

(Below) A block of English billmen of the royal household, tough veterans of the continental wars now fighting for the House of York against the rebel lords. Their equipment is varied, but all have helmets and a breast or jack, and all wear the king's livery colours with various forms of his "sun in splendour" badge. *(Photos Gillian Brook)*

(Above) Man-at-arms and halbardiers, 1470s-80s. The officer is typically armed for dismounted combat with a pollaxe combining an axe blade, a spike, and a broad hammerhead. The halbards are of the shapes common in the Swiss cantons and neighbouring regions. Some have only a blade extended into a thrusting spike; others have a hook on the back of the blade - useful for pulling horsemen out of the saddle, or hooking behind the knee of an opponent on foot.

The Swiss favoured the halbard as their main polearm until the battle of Arbedo in 1422; thereafter they quickly increased the proportion of pikemen. Axemen, halbardiers, and men with two-handed swords were retained in their formations, however. More versatile than pikemen, they often formed the van and rearguard mixed with crossbowmen and handgunners; they also crowded in the centre of the great pike blocks, guarding the banners, and ready to sally out between the files and take offensive action to break a deadlock, or to exploit a beaten

enemy's wavering formation. Given space to fight, the halbard could be swung down at full length like a huge axe. The butchery created by a weapon like a halbard or bill in the hands of a strong, skilled, fast-moving man is horrific to imagine.

(Right) Swiss pikemen wearing the red and white of the city of Thun muster on a bitterly cold March dawn in 1476 before the battle of Grandson. Most Swiss troops were lightly armed; these wear mail and breast plates beneath their outer clothes to keep in body heat - rapidly lost through armour directly exposed to the air.
(Photos John Howe)

(Above & above right)
The German and Italian fight books also give instructions for fighting with pollaxes and halbards, with many cunning moves using blade, point, hook and butt. In the press of battle the halbard's many edges, angles and points must have presented an opponent with a stabbing, hooking, hacking, cork-screwing nightmare of sharp steel.
(Photos Gerry Embleton)

(Right) Pikemen with a mail-clad two-handed swordsman wearing the characteristic turban of the Swiss. This knot of mixed soldiers are fighting in a skirmish in broken terrain, not a pitched battle. While small units of men with cutting weapons could certainly function in a practised team, fighting as individuals but confident in each others' skill and support, pikemen had to act in perfect unison, or the forest of tall shafts above their heads would clash and tangle. One writer described another problem: "Most disagreeable is the vibration of the shaft. I have experienced it myself: when fighting with a long pike it is almost impossible to strike with precision, as the point vibrates too much, particularly when thrust too hard. It vibrates even more when the full length of the weapon is used with the right arm hilly extended. A slow, steady push at a judicious moment is the only method of striking an enemy...on a weak point, the stomach or neck or the articulations of his armour...."
(Photo Carlos Oliveira)

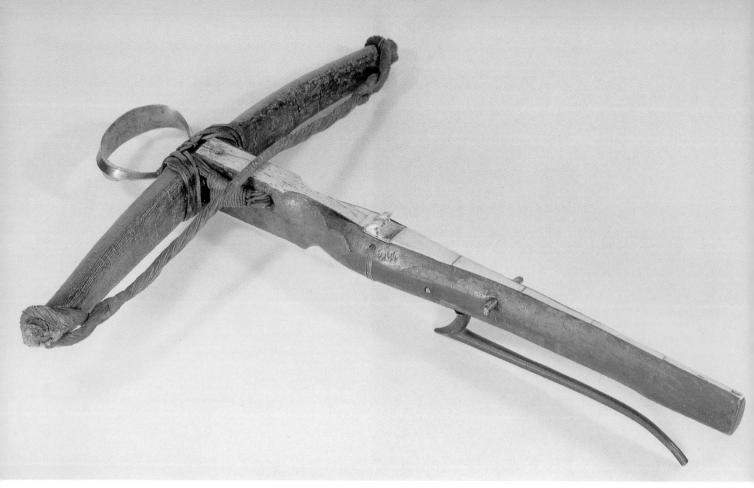

The Crossbow

The crossbow had a similar status in parts of continental Europe to the longbow in Britain. It was a favourite hunting weapon in Germany, Switzerland and parts of Italy. Regular practice was encouraged by competitions and regulations; towns and villages formed shooting clubs, and members paraded proudly with their bows and guild banners - some of these clubs still exist today. Some districts became famous for their crossbowmen, and sent companies to other cities; the Genoese fought for the French at Crécy, and we read that the men of Guyenne "...are courageous, light headed and good men-at-arms, the common people are all crossbowmen." Swiss and German armies frequently fielded mixed companies of crossbowmen and handgunners as skirmishers. Mostly they fought on foot; but the introduction of the cranequin or rack - a compact mechanical spanning device incorporating a winding handle and ratchet - made reloading on horseback possible.

(Above) The crossbow consisted of a short, powerful bowstave mounted crosswise at the end of a wooden stock or "tiller". The stave was originally of composite construction, with wood, horn, whalebone and sinew cunningly fitted and bonded together.

Originally the bowman grounded the stirrup at the end of the stock and placed his foot in it; then knelt, engaging the bowstring with a hook hanging from a stout waistbelt; and straightened up, thus spanning the bow. More powerful crossbows were spanned using various mechanical windlass or leverage devices. The bolt or quarrel was a short, thick wooden arrow with leather or wooden flights set diagonally to spin it in flight. This was shot with great force when the string was released by a trigger mechanism. Armies used vast numbers on campaign - medieval accounts speak of hundreds of thousands of bolts.
(Photo Ian Ashdown)

(Left) A crossbowman wearing a deep kettle hat and breast plate, carrying a steel bow, and with his cranequin slung from his belt. Steel bows were first introduced as early as 1313 and slowly replaced those of composite construction, but saw widespread use only at the end of the 15th century. Very great skill was needed to forge a steel bow that would release the bolt fast and cleanly without a powerful shock; and a contemporary writer noted that they were liable to crack in very cold weather. Note the thick bowstring, made from many strands of cord looped back and forth and bound together.
(Photo Gillian Brooks)

(Above) In a castle just south of the Rhine in 1479 a crossbowman of the garrison waits to go out on patrol. He wears a visored sallet and a breast plate over a thickly padded jacket which protects his shoulders. His clothes and equipment reflect hard service, but his weapons are well cared for. *(Photo John Howe)*

(Above right) This mounted crossbowman, who will act as scout for the patrol, is protected by a light helmet and breast plate; his bow is protected against rain by a laced leather cover, but note that the steel stirrup protrudes. He wears long riding boots held up by tabs and points. *(Photo John Howe)*

(Right) A wooden quiver covered with leather hangs from the crossbowman's belt; note that the bolts are carried point uppermost, the shape of the quiver allowing space for the wooden shafts and flights. Crossbow quivers were usually, though not invariably of this shape, and covered with pigskin or fur; some had lids, and on occasion they bore livery badges or painted decoration. *(Photo John Howe)*

61

(Below) Ready to move out, the foot crossbowman adjusts the cover of his bow. Note the crossed straps across his back which support the breast plate. On his left hip hangs a linen bag, perhaps containing a little bread, cheese and smoked pork.

The crossbow's major advantage over the self or "long" bow was the fact that relatively little training and a reasonably straight eye were all that was needed to turn out a competent bowman. It took no special physical strength, and at moderate ranges its flatter trajectory was easier to predict. Its disadvantage was the time it took to reload. Modern experiments have shown that three shots a minute is good practice when using a cranequin; a windlass is even slower; but four to six shots a minute are possible with a bow spanned by muscle-power and a belt-hook. A practised longbow archer can achieve twice that rate. *(Photo John Howe)*

(Above) A Bernese crossbow-man patrols the walls of his city in the winter of 1476. There is no immediate danger, and he has taken the thick linen bowstring off and stowed it in the bosom of his jacket to keep dry.

We know surprisingly little about the performance of crossbows. Experiments in the 19th century suggest ranges equal or superior to the conventional bow; the inferior flight characteristics of the bolt as compared to the conventional arrow might suggest that accuracy dropped off more quickly, but against this may be set the greater consistency of the mechanical release. At shorter ranges the bolt had great impact and penetration, smashing through mail with ease. *(Photo John Howe)*

The Bow

The longbow (called simply a bow in medieval times, or even an "English" bow, due to the international fame of English archers) was a wooden stave, usually D-shaped in section and tapering at both ends, ideally between 5ft.7ins. and 6ft.2ins. in length. The tips of the bowstave had grooves or fitted horn caps - "nocks" - to take the loops of the hemp string. Yew was the favourite wood, though elm, witch-hazel, ash and others were also used; many yew staves were imported from Italy through Venice. The bowstave - usually made from a branch - employed the red heartwood in the "belly" or inside curve of the bow, and the goldern sapwood on the "back" or outside of the curve; this gave the best combination of compression and elasticity.

Archers

During the 14th and 15th centuries the English archer's pay changed little. On service "out of England" it was 6 pence per day for a mounted archer, 3 pence for a foot archer; for garrison service in England it was respectively 4 pence and 3 pence. Thus a mounted archer earned three times the pay of a skilled civilian worker, a foot archer one and a half times. Many contracts specified that if pay fell in arrears by more than three or six months the contract was null; and bonuses were

frequently paid.

Most archers must have been big, fit men, and the secret of their power was lifelong practice. Successive kings of England had ordered that all able-bodied men should practice regularly: Edward IV's statutes of 1466 order that every Englishman and Irishman between the ages of 16 and 60 should have "an English bow of his own length...." In 1470 official disapproval was voiced against such distractions as "dyce, coytes, tenys...and many new ymagyned games": every healthy man must practice with his bow. As a result, in 1474 King Edward had 14,000 archers under his command.

There was a difference in status between archers recruited in wartime and those permanently retained by the nobility. A good retained archer was well looked after; we read in household accounts of expensive bows, arrows and other equipment provided for them. In 1467 Daniel, one of Sir John Howard's household archers, received an annuity of £10 (cf. the mounted archer's home service rate of £6.08, above), two gowns, a house for his wife, other clothes and sums of money including 20 pence to attend a shooting match. In 1481 Sir John gave Harry Mainwaring and Thomas Cooke sallets, brigandines covered with purple velvet, mail collars, "jacket and gusset", simple arm armour, and sheafs of arrows.

(Left) Archers of Richard of Gloucester's household carrying arrows in their belts; one has the heads secured in a small leather bag. Arrows were almost always carried at the waist, rarely in box-like quivers, and very rarely slung from the shoulder - a position comfortable for travel and hunting but useless for rapid shooting. Illustrations usually show large linen arrow bags, or a sort of tube of cloth enclosing the arrows fixed to the belt, with drawstrings closing both ends. *(Photo Gerry Embleton)*

(Above) In 1577, a century after the great days of the archer, William Harrison lamented: "The French... turn up their tails and cry 'shoot, English!' ...But if some of our Englishmen now lived that served king Edward the third, the breech of such a varlet should have been nailed to his bum, and another feathered in his bowels, before he should have turned about to see who shot the first".

The status and reputation of the archer at the end of the 15th century was such that they were chosen for royal and noble guards: in the 1450s Charles VII of France had a Scottish Archer Guard; and in the 1470s more than a thousand English bowmen served Charles the Bold, forming part of his garde du corps. A Burgundian captain wrote that "The English have been more watched and admired in our army and better esteemed than were our robes of cloth of gold and costly adornments...". *(Photo John Howe)*

Officer and men of Richard of Gloucester's household in 1471. They are as well dressed as one would expect of the bodyguard of a great nobleman, in good woollen cloth in the royal colours of blue and murray, with their master's boar badge embroidered on the breast. They represent the duke's power and guard his person; for war each would have the best helmet, armour, brigandine and weapons that money could buy, and in peace their handsome appearance demonstrates to the world the duke's wealth and generosity. *(Photo Gerry Embleton)*

(Above) Arrows were made from more than a dozen woods, but aspen was preferred, with ash a second choice. The shape of the arrow varied, affecting its performance: parallel-sided, tapered (from the head backward), barrelled (swelling out in the middle), or chested (with the swell set back towards the nock). The latter were the most aerodynamically efficient and were preferred by strong shooters; most arrows found in the wreck of the 16th century *Mary Rose* were tapered. The sheer brute bulk of a medieval war arrow has to be seen to be appreciated.

The feathered flights, usually goose, were 6 to 8ins. long; they were glued and often tied on with a spiral of fine thread. In the 1470s it was directed that six wing feathers from every goose were to be collected throughout the counties and towns of England and sent to London.

The points varied, but the narrow, square-sectioned "bodkin" was ideal for punching through mail and fabric armour. Most arrows were stopped by plate armour even at fairly close range; the angle of impact was vital, but even an arrow striking at 90 degrees would rarely pierce the steel deeply enough to wound seriously. Wounds to less well protected bodies could be many inches deep, doing fatal internal damage (we should recall that Tudor archers recorded shooting arrows clean through an inch of seasoned timber). *(Photo Gerry Embleton)*

Performance

(Below & below right) The range of the bow depends on its power and the strength of the archer. Modern archers have shot bows with draw-weights of 120-160lbs., and no doubt the best of the highly trained medieval bowmen would have bee capable of more. At least one modern archer -John Noonan - regularly attained ranges of 360 yards with an 118-lb. yew bow. In the 16th century Sir John Smythe wrote that war arrows should travel 240 yards, and "then some number of archers being chosen, that could with flights [lighter, long-range arrows] shoot 24 or 20 scores [480 or 400 yards], as there be many that can...." Shakespeare speaks of 290 yards as a good shot; and a list of 17th century archery practice grounds gives lengths up to 380 yards.

Numbers and speed were far more important in battle than mere range, however. Expert Burgundian writers of the day, who had seen the English in action, used them as a figure of speech, speaking of shot flying "thicker than arrows in an English battle"; and stating, "I am of the opinion that the most important thing in the world in battle is archers, but they must be in thousands, for in small numbers they do not prevail." Ten shots in a minute was a steady rate of shooting; the modern archer Clive Bartlett, shooting a 70lb. bow, has managed 15 in a minute, all of which landed within a 12-foot square area at a range of 300 paces. It was this "barrage" shooting which made the English truly deadly; a thousand archers could pour a hail of 10,000 to 12,000 shafts down on their foe every minute - and field armies typically had several thousand archers. *(Photos David Gallagher, Alan & Michael Perry)*

Supply

There are references to different types of arrows - long range "flight" arrows, and heavier types - with different lengths of fletchings. An archer probably had his own favourite arrows, more expensive than "army issue". He was expected to arrive for service with a "sheaf" of 24 or 30; and might go into action with two sheaves, giving him four or five minutes' shooting. It is clear that immense reserves were necessary, and contemporary documents describe them in detail. In 1359, for instance, 20,000 bows, 850,000 arrows and 50,000 bowstrings were gathered at the Tower of London; and a 1475 supply list mentions 10,060 "sheffes" - more than a quarter of a million arrows.

Bow production was a well established industry. Staves came from carefully tended plantations of pollarded trees. Royal statutes controlled and encouraged the trade: Edward IV's statute of 1472 is typical. Every vessel sailing for England from "any other city, town, or country from whence any such bowstaves have been before this time bought" must bring in four bowstaves for each ton of merchandise. The numbers were carefully checked and the imports marked for quality; and the staves-not yet shaped into finished bows-must be "three fingers thick and squared, seven feet long, to be well got up, polished and without knots".

It might take a skilled bowyer about one and three-quarter hours to turn a stave into a bow costing no more than 3 shillings 4 pence (by royal order, in 1475). These were "livery" bows - army issue; the personal bow of a household archer might cost double that. In time of war an army of fletchers, bowyers and smiths would turn out bows and arrows by the ton; once again, we are reminded that organisation on this scale cannot have been simple or "primitive".

(It is pleasant to note that among those who made arrows for Lord Howard's household was one "Robard Hoode", from whom eight "shafttys" were bought on 26 September 1465.)

Finally, an eyewitness description from a disinterested foreign

observer: "...There is hardly any without a helmet and none without bows and arrows: their bows and arrows are thicker and longer than those used by other nations, just as their bodies are stronger than other peoples', for they seem to have hands and arms of iron. The range of their bows is no less than that of our arbalests [crossbows]; there hangs by the side of each a sword no less long than ours, but heavy and thick as well. The sword is always accompanied by an iron shield [buckler]...They do not wear any metal armour on their breast... the common soldiery have more comfortable tunics that reach down below the loins and are stuffed with tow or some other soft material...." (Dominic Mancini, 1483)

(Right) "...We found all the archers with their boots off and with a stake driven into the ground before them, and there were many barrels of wine broached for them to drink. From the small amount which I saw I have never seen men

more willing to fight...." Thus Commynes described Burgundian archers before the battle of Montlhery; there were many excellent archers serving in continental armies, all but eclipsed from memory by the dazzling performance of the English.

The French raised companies of bowmen; and it is little known that many Frenchmen were recruited into English archer companies in France. The Flemish archers were sometimes mixed with crossbowmen. A muster roll of 1476 notes that Hainault and the Somme each supplied about 1,000 foot archers to the Duke of Burgundy's army, and Artois, 1,289 archers and pikes.

This man wears a Burgundian livery jacket in the colours prescribed by the Abbeville ordinance of July 1471, and is dressed for a practice shoot, without his armour; for grip in the mud he has taken off his shoes and rolled up his footless hose. *(Photo John Howe)*

ARTILLERY

Burgundian artillery open fire on troops from the garrison of one of the chain of castles along the foot of the Jura mountains marking the frontier of Vaud and Burgundian territories. Swiss raids into this area in 1475 led to a particularly bloody series of clashes; in 1476 the Burgundian army returned to the offensive.

(Inset) A youthful artillery assistant, hooded against the drizzle, sponges out the hot barrel after a discharge, while the gunner blows on his match. *(Photos John Howe)*

Gunpowder

Some time early in the 14th century gunpowder reached the battlefields of Europe. Cannon and handguns were seen in increasing numbers, their adoption more rapid on the continent than in England. By the mid-15th century most major powers possessed considerable arsenals, and towns throughout Europe were stockpiling guns and powder. In 1413 John the Fearless of Burgundy bought 10,000lbs. of powder, saltpetre and sulphur; in 1425 Henry VI of England's marshal in France used 12,600lbs. on campaign; by the 1470s we read of more than 189,000lbs. stored in arsenals in the state of Milan. In Germany, France, Italy and Burgundy artillery pieces in their thousands ate up a major share of the military budgets of their day.

A surviving list of the French King Louis XI's artillery in the 1470s illustrates the scale of the military effort required of an army wishing to deploy a serious artillery train:

"For the bombard called 'Orleans' or 'La Realle' - 41 horses.

"Other bombards - between 13 and 31 horses each.

"For various serpentines - 12 to 14 horses.

"For 8 faulcons [captured by the Burgundians and used by them at the siege of Beauvais, 1472] - 2 horses each.

"For 2 forges and their equipment - 12 horses.

"For gunpowder, saltpetre, sulphur, charcoal and equipment for making gunpowder - 276 horses.

"For lead - 129 horses; and for 200,000 shot (mostly small) - 600 horses."

The French artillery were organised into *bandes*, under a *capitaine de la bande*. According to the French ordinance of 1411, master-gunners were generally independent artisans organised in "corporations" who might be hired for a siege or campaign, sometimes serving groups of guns, sometimes a single piece. Gunners were free to recruit auxiliaries, apprentices, or their own families to serve the guns. We know the names of some: Master Girault de Samien served the Burgundian guns at the siege of Paris; and Charles the Bold paid no less than £50 to the wife and family of his hired gunner Master Hans of Nuremberg while Hans was away on campaign.

Fixed ammunition

We do not know when cartridges were first used. Many historians maintain that they did not predate the 17th century; yet in his great work Pyrotechnia written in the 1530s, Vannoccio Biringuccio (1480-C.1539) described in detail the two ways to load a muzzle-loading cannon:

"In order to load the guns, make an instrument which gunners call a loading ladle." [He describes a semi-cylindrical sheet iron or copper ladle, three times as long as the diameter of the ball and corresponding to half the circumference of the muzzle, mounted on a pole.] The ladle "full of powder is put in the gun and carries it to the end. Then, turning the hand over, it is emptied inside and the powder is struck with the foot of the pole, which presses and sends it into place." His second method is the first detailed description of cartridge:

"Guns are also loaded in another way, which experts call the cartridge method. A tube is made of paper folded two or three times and wrapped on a round piece of wood as long and thick as you think is required....This is closed at the foot and filled with all the powder that it can contain. Then it is put in the gun with the said ladle and pushed so hard with the rammer that it bursts and scatters the powder....Then the wad of hay is put in and after that the ball, as you did in the others....Using this method is a very quick way. For this, a number of these cartridges are kept made up and also filled."

The Swiss chronicles of the 1480s and 1490s clearly show ammunition boxes containing powder charges and shot in separate compartments - both for large guns and, remarkably, for handguns. A manuscript drawn about 1505 and now in the Württemberg Landesbibliothek in Stuttgart clearly shows a cartridge made of paper or cloth - which also appears to contain the ball; an inscription comments that this is a "rapid method".

Mop, ladle, rammer and linstock are all visible in many 15th century illustrations. Shot guages were made by tracing and cutting a hole the size of the gun's bore in a wooden board. In March 1432 the English council at Rouen wrote to Governor Vernon asking him to purchase gun stones "of the size and measure of which we send you the form in a loop", for use in the siege of the tower of Rouen.

The powder charge for breech-loaders was placed in a separate, roughly tankard-shaped iron breech chamber, of which two or three were supplied for each gun, and secured with a hammered wooden tompion; the ball was placed in the barrel, and the breech wedged home behind it. Recent experiments have shown that breech-loaders could be fired very rapidly - two to three shots per minute is not a difficult rate. There is no reason to think that late 15th century mobile campaign artillery was significantly slower to load and fire than that of the 18th or early 19th century. During a siege a gunner took his time; threatened with attack, he no doubt speeded up impressively.

(Above left & above) Two breech-loading Burgundian guns in action; note the large flash of flame from the priming, and the thick white smoke rising from muzzle and breech. A great deal of gas compression is inevitably lost through the approximate fit between the wedged breech and the rear lip of the barrel. Even so, recent experiments with stone and iron balls achieved surprising accuracy over several hundred yards. With Napoleonic iron balls of only approximate size leaving considerable "windage", one of these guns achieved a three-round group just over a metre across at 300 metres range with a virtually flat trajectory.

Note the hand-gunners in support; guns of all shapes and sizes, and crossbows, were deemed "artillery" in the 15th century. *(Photos John Howe)*

(Right) Burgundian gun crew at practice on a wet day. Modern experiments have been particularly successful in firing cannon in wet weather - if the touchhole is kept covered and the gun is primed and fired briskly the powder will ignite in all but the heaviest rain. Contemporary accounts give the impression that gun "crews" were surprisingly small, with one man only, or one to several guns; but these of course refer only to the gunner himself - other documents make clear that there were enough "assistants" to serve the guns properly. *(Photo Philippe Krauer / L'Illustré)*

The loading drill for a late 15th century breech-loading gun:

(Above) The touchhole ot one of the separate breeches is cleaned. When a measured charge of powder has been poured in from a prepared bag, the breech is sealed with a hammered softwood tompion. The breech is engaged with the rear lip of the barrel; and a sturdy iron-bound wedge is inserted and hammered home behind the breech. The ball would now be inserted from the muzzle.

(Right) The touchhole is primed with powder from a horn. The crew stand clear, and a smouldering match is touched to the priming. In the last picture incandescent grains of powder can be seen blown back from the breech. We may assume that in 15th century armies - as in modern reconstruction experiments - the gunner is readily identifiable by small burnt holes all over the front and sleeves of his doublet... *(Photos John Howe)*

(Above left) Swiss artillery in action during the 1470s. The gunner with the linstock, centre, wears the black and white colours of the town of Fribourg, an ally of Berne; he has stripped to doublet and hose for the hot work of serving the guns.
(Photo John Howe)

(Left) Terms used for categories of cannon varied depending upon which clerk wrote them down; there was no real standardisation from country to country. Guns in the Burgundian service described as *regulaires* could be anything from 3ft. to 10ft. long, with bores of from 2ins. to 10ins.; some were muzzle-loaders, some breech-loaders. *Couleuvrines* seem to have been from 2ft. to 4ft. long, with bores of 3ins. to 4ins.; the term covered large guns mounted on carriages and small hand-held weapons. *Serpentines,* both muzzle-and breech-loading, between 3ft.6ins. and 7ft. long and with bores of 2ins. to 6ins., could be mounted on wheeled carriages. The muzzle-loader illustrated - an English reconstruction - would be described as a serpentine. There were as many different types of carriage as of barrels in this period of lively experimentation; note here the double elevation arcs.
(Photo Gillian Brooks)

Bombards

Bombards came in many sizes, but at their largest these great "wallbreaker" guns might be described in strategic terms as the "nuclear weapons" of their age: by owning them a prince demonstrated his wealth and power - and his ability to batter his way into the castle of any rebellious nobleman. Pulled slowly across country by huge teams of horses and supported by an immense train, they were obviously an impressive spectacle; but they were also formidable weapons. Despite their ponderous appearance they were not clumsy or crude: neither the craftsmen who made them, nor the princes who poured out a river of gold to own them, were fools. In 1411 an eyewitness described the Burgundians setting up one of their biggest bombards, "called Griete", outside the main gate of Bourges, capital of the Duchy of Berry:

"It shot stones of enormous weight at the cost of quantities of gunpowder and much hard and dangerous work on the part of its expert crew. Nearly twenty men were required to handle it. When it was fired the thunderous noise could be heard tour miles away, and terrorised the local inhabitants as if it were

some reverberation from Hell. On the first day, the foundations of one of the towers were partly demolished by a direct hit. On the next day this cannon fired twelve stones, two of which penetrated the tower, thus exposing many of the buildings and their inhabitants."

One wonders if this gun could have been *Dulle Griet*, five metres (16ft.5ins.) long and with a bore of 64cm (25ins.), which stands today on the bank of the river Leie in Ghent; she is the largest surviving bombard. The Duke of Brabant was said to have had one 35-ton monster forged in 1409-1411. The famous *Mons Meg* which stands today at Edinburgh Castle is 404cm (13ft.3ins.) long, with a bore of 19.6ins., and weighs 6040kg (nearly 6 tons). Her barrel is made of hoops and staves of iron, the powder chamber of small pieces of iron hammer-welded together.

Understandably, no firing tests have been attempted with surviving bombards, so we know little of their performance. In the reign of Mary Queen of Scots *Mons Meg* is supposed to have fired her three-hundredweight shot (336lbs., 152kg) out to two miles. In 1571 a crew fired her

24 times in two and a half hours - just over six minutes per shot: so much for the curious modern idea that such guns took hours to prepare and load.

Bombards were often used as close to the enemy's walls as possible, with smaller cannon firing in concert, the crews protected by large wooden mantlets; thus, a Burgundian *maitre de bombard* also commanded a sort of battery of supporting pieces.
(Photo Philippe Krauer/L'Illustré)

Handguns

The ancestor of the relatively sophisticated matchlocks in use by the end of the 15th century was the simple gun tube mounted on a stout pole. Powder and ball were inserted, wadded and rammed home; priming powder was poured into and around the touchhole in the top of the breech, and touched off by hand with a smouldering match or heated wire - this was, literally, a hand cannon. Many differing examples of this rudimentary weapon, varying greatly in size, saw widespread use throughout the century, particularly for the defence of castles and towns. The lighter pieces became increasingly practical.

By the middle of the 15th century a more sophisticated system was in common use. The touchhole was moved to the side of the barrel and a small external pan, with a pivotting cover, was fixed around it to hold the priming. The barrel was now mounted in a practically-shaped shoulder-stock, no doubt inspired by that of the crossbow. A simple S-shaped lever was fitted to the stock, holding a piece of smouldering saltpetre-soaked cord clamped to its upper end. When the lower part of the lever was

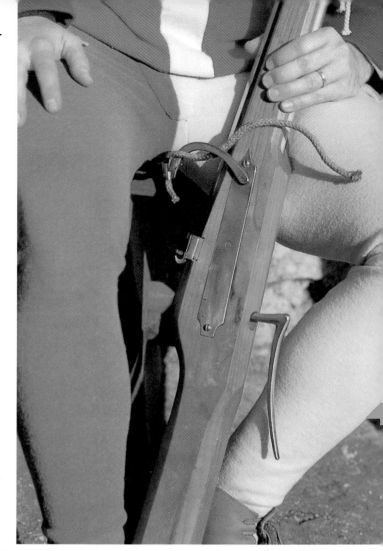

squeezed upwards the top end descended, bringing the end of the match into the priming. Further development led to the appearance, by the 1470s, of more efficient matchlocks with the "cock" operated by a spring-loaded release.

The Swiss chronicles clearly show handgunners aiming with weapons both resting on top of the shoulder, and tucked into the shoulder in the modem manner. Ramrods are sometimes visible fixed beneath the barrel; powder is earned in gourds and horns, and shot in pouches. In one case a small two-compartment ammunition box is shown, with separate powder charges and balls. Mixed forces of handgunners and crossbowmen acted as skirmishers, and examples of their small flags-bearing a bow on one side and a gun on the other - survive in Swiss collections.

Many individuals owned guns. In 1431 the council of Frankfurt on Main decreed that every citizen capable of bearing arms had to have a gun - some 2,000 in all. By 1444 they ordered that there should be two handguns and a small breech-loader for each of 1,000 war-wagons. A muster of 523 citizens of Neuchâtel in 1470 shows 100 with their own guns.

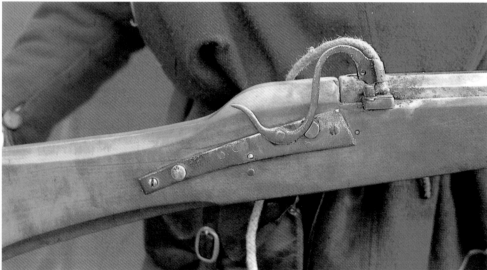

(Above) The direct ancestor of the 17th century matchlock: a lever-released mechanism clearly visible in the Swiss chronicles and various German sources of the 1480s-90s. The division of the "cock" into two parts, the upper part holding the match being operated by a spring release concealed behind the plate in the side of the stock, was presumably a development of the earlier crossbow mechanism, in which the string was held back by a rotating nut which was released by pressure on an external lever.
(Photo Gerry Embleton)

(Left) An alternative button release, showing the S-shaped cock - the lower curve was used to pull it back and cock it - and the press-button, left, which released the internal spring catch mounted inside the metal plate. Note the length of the match, which had to be kept smouldering in action and was consumed at a considerable rate; and the grey fouling of burnt powder around the touchhole.
(Photo Gerry Embleton)

(Below left) A surprisingly modern-looking gunlock, based on a German manuscript possibly as early as the 1470s. Note the rear sight fixed to the barrel.
(Photo John Howe)

(Above & right) Summer 1476: skirmishers of the Burgundian army meet Swiss scouts from the garrison of Murten as Duke Charles moves up to lay siege to the town... Increasingly large numbers of handgunners saw service with European field armies as the century drew towards its close. Like the crossbow, the handgun required little training and no particular strength; and its ammunition was relatively cheap.

An old-fashioned concept of the knightly ideal and the privileges of the high-born did not sit comfortably with a weapon which could make any humble soldier as dangerous as a noble man-at-arms - and at considerably greater range. Some had long considered it dishonourable to put crossbowmen - who did not even need the strength and skill-at-arms of archers - into the field against their betters, and the Pope had tried in vain to ban their use against any but infidels. Gunpowder was clearly the work of Satan; the Florentine commander Gian Paolo Vitelli was far from alone in his attitude when, taking the castle of Buti in 1498, he had the hands of captured gunners cut off and their eyes put out....
(Photos John Howe)

The Burgundian ordinance of Bohain en Vermandois, 13 November 1472, laid down that a handgunner had to have a mailshirt, a *gorgerin* (mail or plate protection for the throat), breast plate and sallet; he should carry gun, sword and dagger. This handgunner, out scouting, follows many contemporary illustrations in being very lightly protected, perhaps wearing only a mailshirt under his jacket. His clothes have been given him by the knight he serves; and he wears over all the livery described in an ordinance of 1471 and worn by all the duke's forces, even when serving the King of France. He carries a ration bag, a gourd for powder, and a leather bullet bag, the cord sling passing through and holding closed two wooden slats at its mouth. *(Photos John Howe)*

CASTLES AND SIEGES

Sieges were a long and serious undertaking. No one but a Hollywood film director would storm a fortress by rushing undamaged defences with scaling ladders in broad daylight. Whenever possible the garrison would be persuaded to surrender, or starved into submission. Very often a traitor would be bribed to let the attackers in – by far the most cost-effective method. The taking of a powerful fortress or walled town, provisioned and strongly garrisoned, was a hugely expensive project not lightly to be undertaken.

Once committed to an attempt the attackers had to assemble massive siege trains, engineers, workmen, supplies, and enough troops both to envelop the fortress and to beat off any relieving army which might appear. The arrival of such an overwhelming display of force might persuade the garrison to capitulate at once or after an honourable interval, when they might be allowed to march out with all the "honours of war". If they refused to deliver up the castle they faced weeks, months, or even years of hunger, hardship and dwindling numbers, probably ending in massacre.

An idea of the vast and complex organisation of a major siege, backed by production on an industrial scale, may be found in the popular *Book of Armes and of Chyvalrye* written in French in 1408–09 by Christine de Pisan,

and printed in English by Caxton in 1489. Under the heading "of leyenge of a syege and of sawtyngys of fortresses" she listed all the arms and equipment needed by the attacking force over six months:

The best time to attack is at harvest, when the attackers can deprive the defenders of vital supplies and benefit themselves. Proclamations must be made in the surrounding villages forbidding trade with the besieged, and encouraging it with the besiegers. Vast quantities of timbers, wagons, horses and oxen are necessary, and if moving by water then barges, boats, and a crane to unload them.

A barricade must be constructed completely surrounding the fortress, nearly one and a half miles long, built of 540 wooden panels 14ft. long by 12ft. high, with gates and wooden towers. A barn 144ft. by 48ft. must be built for the horse-powered flour mills and other equipment. Mantlets for the guns must be constructed on an immense scale – 31 in all, the largest 12ft. by 30ft. by 2ft. thick. For the seven-man crews of four great catapults mantlets 18ft. by 36ft. and 6ins. thick are needed.

Over 3,000 carpenters and labourers should be recruited, many of them also archers, with ropemakers, wheelwrights, and turners to make elmwood tompions to place between powder and ball in the guns. A

total of 248 guns should be assembled, including "two great bombards, four lesser bombards and 33 great guns"; 30,000lbs. of gunpowder, 2,200 stones, 6,000lbs. of lead, 200,000 crossbow quarrels, and 1,200 paveses. Double ladders "wyth grete hokes of yron that shall a grype the batellments", 1,000 shovels, 200 lanterns, barrels with locks and keys, tallow to lubricate wheels...The list goes on and on; and why should it surprise us – how else could one attack the massive and sophisticated fortifications that still dominate our landscape today?

Medieval siege literature is not all as ponderously sensible as Christine de Pisan's manual. One hardly knows how to react to a passage from Taccola's *The Art of War* (c. 1450) in which he recommends introducing incendiary cats into drains or breaches to burn down wooden buildings – or "if there is a shortage of cats one should take mice..."

Philippe de Croy, a captain in Charles the Bold's army besieging Neuss in 1474, left an account of daily life – for one of fairly privileged rank – in the snow-bound siege lines (quoted here from *Charles the Bold* by Richard Vaughan):

" ...The thunder of the two bombards and their fumes in which we are cured are not musical instruments nor do they

make a cordial syrup. Shot from hackbuts and culverins flies at us thicker than arrows in an English battle.... I am lodged in an abbey...where there are small rooms and lodgings.... In this place I can daily experience a great many of the abuses of this world, because in some [rooms] here, through excess of money, games and gambling go on all day long, and in others, in default [of money], there is only dinner. Some sing and play flutes and other instruments, others weep and regret their dead relatives or even their own infirmity. On one side I hear the cheery cry 'A right royal drink!'; on the other, 'Jesus', to encourage those who are in the last agony of death. There are whores in some rooms; in others the cross which leads the lifeless body to the grave..."

(Photo Gerry Embleton)

Castle and town garrisons were usually spared if they surrendered without resistance – sometimes to the disappointment of their attackers. It has been one of the most ancient and universal laws of war, however, that a garrison who refuse the offer of terms, and force their attackers to face the bloody cost of prolonged siege and final assault, can expect no mercy. In medieval times political policy usually dictated their fate. If the victorious lord saw local advantage in gaining a magnanimous reputation then his vengeance might be limited and selective, and he would hold his men back from more than casual butchery. If he wished to make an example, then the fate of the defeated was swift and cruel. Liege rebelled against Burgundian rule in 1468: its population were massacred, its walls flattened and its houses burned. Nesle in Vermandois shared the same fate in 1472; an eyewitness wrote: "The town was attacked and captured and the majority of its inhabitants killed. Those who were taken alive were hanged, except for a few whom the men-at-arms allowed to escape out of pity, and a large number had their heads chopped off. It upsets me to recount this cruelty, but I was on the spot and I must say something about it..."

(Right) 1476: from a tower of besieged Grandson castle on Lake Neuchâtel, one of the Swiss garrison takes aim at an enemy officer. The Swiss had a long tradition of encouraging marksmanship, and sniping was a common feature of siege warfare. When Grandson finally surrendered Duke Charles put the garrison to death; this horrified the Swiss – though the year before they themselves had massacred most of the population of the Savoyard town of Estavayer just across the lake, beheading the men and drowning women and children. When Swiss chroniclers described a garrison being "thrown out" of a castle by their soldiers, they meant from the top of the battlements.
(Photo Philippe Krauer/ L'Illustré)

(Below) The master gunner of a great fortress watches the construction of the first siegeworks below. This is a well supplied castle, powerfully garrisoned; there is much which can be done to hamper the besiegers – countermines, cunningly placed guns, new defences, sallies to destroy siegeworks and tools – and in time disease may come to stalk through the crowded siege camp.
(Photo Martin Render)

The attackers have broken through an outer gatehouse, and are swarming into the castle; the defenders in the towers and the strong wooden penthouses surmounting the walls turn their fire inwards, fighting desperately with whatever comes to hand. The attackers will suffer heavy loss as they crowd through narrow entranceways; but the garrison's prospects are grim – they can hope for no mercy in the end. *(Photos John Howe, Gerry Embleton)*

Shields and Paveses

Shields were no longer normally used in knightly combat in the 15th century, the development of full armour giving sufficient protection. Exceptions were the round, oval, or kidney-shaped shields still favoured by some Italian and Spanish troops, who retained a light cavalry tradition; the bucklers of the infantry; and the much larger free-standing *paveses* which protected crossbowmen and handgunners at sieges and in static battle lines. Paveses could be highly decorated objects waist-or chest-high, designed as much for display as for combat; or they could be very businesslike defences. Up to two metres high, slightly curved, two or three inches thick and immensely strong, they were usually of wood covered with hide and painted in heraldic colours. Man-sized plain, flat boards were also very widely used as mobile defences in siege lines. The larger paveses often had triangular holes cut at eye-level for vision and shooting. Some had hooks and rings down the edges so that they could be linked in rows; nearly all had either attached supporting props, and/or ground spikes on the bottom edge.

(Above) An English soldier well equipped for the clouds of missiles which he may face at short range during siege work, with a deep sallet, bevor and breast plate worn beneath his livery jacket.
(Photo Alan & Michael Perry)

(Right) An English crossbowman during the Wars of the Roses, sheltering from a rain of arrows from his faster-shooting enemies as he spans his bow with a cranequin. His stout pavese is painted with the Yorkist colours and badges of his master, King Edward IV. Medieval man could not long resist a tempting undecorated surface; paveses were a popular ground for displaying the heraldic colours or arms of a lord or city, and were sometimes beautifully painted with images of the saints.
(Photo David Gallagher)

Pioneers

Well-organised groups of pioneers, called "men of the camp", usually handled siege works and camp construction. Most serious commanders were expected to be well versed in siegecraft; but no doubt there were lesser specialists who had earned good reputations and were sought-after for their skills. The Burgundians had 1,000 pioneers, each wearing a sallet and a "jack with a red St.Andrew's cross on the breast", and all the necessary craftsmen to build fortifications, cut stone and make bridges. To the siege of Paris in 1469 they took "seven or eight small boats brought on carts and many wine-barrel staves to make a bridge over the Seine..."; at daybreak, "a large number of coopers were sent to make barrels from the wood which had been brought...", and by noon the river was bridged. For the same purpose they also carried leather boats with collapsible wooden frames, and illustrations of these and other portable pontoons are to be found in surviving documents.

(Left & above) A pioneer of the Burgundian advance guard in the woods about the castle of Vaumarcus on Lake Neuchâtel, March 1476. He is well armoured, and wears a thick gown against the cold, the sleeves slit to free his arms for work.

The duke's army have taken the castle of Grandson and executed its garrison. A Swiss army is advancing from Neuchâtel, and now the Burgundians have taken Vaumarcus, which stands in the enemy's path; Duke Charles's pioneers are constructing an earthwork to block another track over the ridge above Vaumarcus. *(Photos John Howe)*

(Right) "I looked up at the east at the high sun,
And saw a tower on a toft artfully fashioned,
A deep dale was beneath with a dungeon in it,
And deep ditches and dark, dreadful to see..."
– from William Langland's 'The Vision of Piers Plowman'.

(Photo Claude Huyghens & Françoise Danrigal)

It is difficult to picture how castles must have appeared in the 15th century, and to imagine the lives that were led within them, if we allow our eyes to stop short at the ruins which brood over British landscapes. But many German and Swiss castles have remained in almost constant use over the centuries; and although they now house museums or government offices, their glazed windows, white outer walls and plastered interiors are in fact nearer to their original appearance than the slighted ruins which are all that remain of most British castles.

To recreate a living castle in our mind's eye from these stone bones we must add the flesh that has withered away – and above all, colour. We must top the walls with projecting wooden hoardings, the tile or slate roofs bright and complete, the great walls lime-washed. We must coat the interior walls with fresh plaster, often painted to imitate regular courses of ashlars; in important rooms the plaster must be covered with colourful decorative patterns, or rich hangings. We must add doors and curtains to block the

draughts; shutter or glaze the windows; light roaring fires in the many hearths; and furnish the rooms with glowing wood. We must add busy kitchens; in some castles we must install tapped water, piped from rain tanks in the towers.

Although wars swept back and forth across Europe like the plague, we must remember that there were peaceful times; sometimes certain areas lay relatively untroubled for many years, even generations. In the 15th century there were both brand new castles and ancient, ruinous keeps. Many were family homes, very humble or breathtakingly splendid depending on the owner's purse and taste. Some were of little military importance, some great seats of power sitting across vital lines of trade and communication. Some were garrisoned by little more than a caretaker force; in 1411, just 27 *écuyers* (squires), 26 crossbowmen and three cannoneers were thought sufficient guard for no less than eight French castles, one of which housed just one squire and a single crossbowman.

The military stores of even an important castle could be in

lamentable condition. In 1343 Dover, guarding England's most vulnerable gateway to France, was in a sorry state: the armoury was full of obsolete equipment – bascinets covered in rotten leather, 25 rusty coats of mail, 25 "antique" gauntlets, six buckets of featherless arrows.... However, in many other cases equipment was complete, in great quantity and good repair; and the garrisons, although frequently smaller than one might suppose, were entirely adequate for defence, and in wartime both active and aggressive.

Garrison troops might be professional soldiers –"foreigners" who were the bane of the local people's lives - or locals themselves, with their own trades to follow in their spare time. For a castle to work effectively as a base from which to control the countryside part of its garrison must be mounted men. Foot soldiers could normally cover an area within three to four miles of their base, arriving at its outer edge within an hour of an alarm; mounted men could respond much faster and double the distance covered. Castles are often

found built near enough to one another for their effective areas of control to touch, or nearly so.
(Photo Philippe Krauer/ L'Illustré)

(Right) 1480: the wife of the commander of a great castle in Alsace checks her household linen in the private apartments. Even when the castle's primary function was military many castellans installed their families, and those of the garrison soldiers; in times of peace the normal atmosphere of a household would have prevailed - the little community, enclosed by the walls, must have found ways of rubbing along together on a daily basis it life was to be tolerable. The commander's lady might take over much of the domestic administration - and even, in his absence, the direction of the defence

(Below right) The commander of a small and relatively relaxed garrison does his accounts, while one of his gunners mends his clothes. They are sharing the kitchen - the wannest place on a chilly winter morning.
(Photos Claude Huyghens & Françoise Danrigal)

(Left & above) During the long periods of inactivity normal life must have carried on, much like that of a village; soldiers lived in the castle - courted, married, fathered children, cooked, ate, worked on civilian jobs and repairs to the defences. Their morale and wellbeing - like that of a ship's crew - must have depended on their commander's temperament: there must have been "happy" garrisons, and some near mutiny.
(Photos Philippe Krauer /L'Illustré, John Howe)

Sanitation and Hygiene

(Left) The idea of the occupants of a massive, white-painted, fully furnished castle, seat of power and family home of a wealthy nobleman, all queuing up to use one filthy, draughty latrine in an inaccessible tower is clearly ridiculous. Traces of latrines will usually be found in most sections of a castle; blocks of multi-seaters, often built of timber and thus no longer surviving, were provided for the troops. Some castles, like Dirleton in Northumberland, have a latrine adjacent to every major chamber. The unpleasant and dangerous effects of inadequate sanitation were well understood. Hay, scraps of paper and linen, and probably a wash basin served the purpose of toilet paper. Many illustrations of the bedrooms of all classes show chamber-pots.

The quality of waste disposal facilities and services in towns, and presumably in castles, must have varied from the efficient to the unspeakable. Public and private latrines were built over running water or substantial sewers. Some towns made provision for collecting "nightsoil" for use as fertilizer. *(Photo Suzanne Hupfer)*

Washing and Bathing

Standards of personal hygiene varied, but the idea that medieval people rarely washed and lived in a sea of filth is absurd. There were no doubt many whose only serious encounter with water was at their christening or if they fell into a river; in certain regions splashing water on the body was no doubt considered a dangerous eccentricity; but many 15th century towns provided substantial public bathhouses, which argues a widespread demand. The provision of a bath for guests was a recognised feature of hospitality; to keep relatively clean and sweet was not only healthy and aesthetically pleasing, but helped to keep fleas and lice at bay - an important consideration, given the number of recipes for repelling them found in contemporary household books.

This was also a contributary encouragement to the widespread habit of changing one's linen frequently with or without an accompanying wash, and of using bedsheets. Because of the difficulty of cleaning woollen blankets and quilts even the poor, household servants and peasants used sheets on their beds. Records show that Sir John Falstoff's castle at Caister had separate bedrooms for the cook, gardener, porter and other servants, with feather beds, fustian blanket, two sheets, bolster, coverlet and curtain.

(Left) Sometimes refugees flocked to the fortified places; often travellers or passing troops would be given shelter. Here, in spring 1475, a camp kitchen has been set up between the outer and inner walls to feed a company of allies, soldiers on their way to join the Emperor's army mustering to relieve the besieged city of Neuss near Cologne. *(Photo Claude Huyghens & Françoise Danrigal)*

(Right) A sentry shelters from the sun the gatehouse of a fortress in northern Spain, 1468. Unremitting vigilance was necessary to keep the roof over one's head and the breath in one's body during constant petty wars. His dress and equipment are identical to those of his northern brothers - indeed, many English and German mercenaries served in the Spanish wars. *(Photo John Howe)*

THE ARMIES

To describe in detail the 15th century military history and status of an entire continent and the organisation of its armies is obviously beyond the scope of this book. We can only sketch in a few basic facts, and give an impression of the different characteristics of some of the major military powers. Their organisation was broadly similar, differing only in detail and in the terms used.

Roughly, every property-owner owed military service to his "landlord", protector or town. He was expected to come armed and equipped for war when called, with appropriate numbers of followers, or to pay others to serve in his stead. The wealthier and more powerful the individual the more followers he was expected to provide. Whatever their theoretical organisation, the strength of medieval armies actually depended largely on who could or would turn out for service and what he could bring with him.

Horse and foot were usually organised into "lances" - administrative rather than tactical units, each lance consisting of a man-at-arms and a number of mounted and foot followers, variously armoured and armed. These might be organised into companies of various sizes and names, and thence into larger formations. Similarly armed and equipped men were grouped together in tactical units for battle. Blocks of footsoldiers were usually organised into tens, twenties, thirties, fifties and hundreds under junior officers or "NCOs" - *disenier, vingtainier* ("vintner" in England), *centenier,* etc.

In practice the remnants of the old feudal military system were, by the 15th century, usually inadequate to raise armies of sufficient size, consistency, quality, or availability (since service was generally subject to strict time limitations). In consequence most armies included significant numbers of mercenaries, usually foreigners, hired for pay through professional commanders under the terms of straightforward commercial contracts. While the home forces called up for military service were commanded by the local aristocracy, and the newly powerful town militias by their bishops, councils, guild-masters and bourgeoisie (of widely varying leadership qualities), the mercenaries were normally led by experienced professionals.

Each monarch and powerful aristocrat maintained household bodyguard troops - varying in size from a handful of archers to a small army. The forces of the state were usually divided between a field army and first- and second-class reserves, the latter a rural "home guard" to be mustered only in grave emergency.

Flags and Uniforms
There was an established code, varying considerably in each kingdom, governing the size and shape of flags proper to each rank of the nobility, but these were not always followed: the medieval world loved display, and strict standardisation was an alien concept. Flags of every description were adapted to decorate castles and tents, to indicate rank and military formation, and to please the eye. Certain heraldic devices and colours, varying with each artist, paint-supplier and dyer, were more or less strictly adhered to; but secondary badges and colours were frequently adopted and changed at whim, and used very freely to embellish clothes, pavilions and possessions of all kinds.

The Duke of Nevers, in nominal command of Christendom's great effort against the Turks in 1396 (which ended in disastrous defeat at Nicopolis), equipped his personal company, 200 strong, all in "gaygreen" livery, with green satin tents, new banners, pennons, tabards and trumpet banners, all embroidered with the figure of the Virgin on a field powdered with the lilies of France and the arms of Nevers and Burgundy. In 1414 the 17-year-old Dauphin of France, in "a jovial mood", had a "handsome standard made, covered in beaten gold and adorned with a K, a swan, and an L" - for no more reason than that there was a pretty girl in the queen's household whose emblems these were.

We have many records of "uniform" clothing being worn - far more than is generally accepted. It might take the form of an issue of cloth as part of the normal "livery", usually made annually to retainers; or of garments specially made up for a campaign or festive event. Guild members were proud to wear hoods or other clothes in their guild colours, and when serving together as soldiers they would form a uniformly-dressed contingent. Lords or towns might dress their soldiers entirely in their colours, and identifying scarves,

feathers, livery jackets and badges were generally worn.

The "national" crosses of St. George and St.Andrew were worn by whole English and Burgundian armies, as was the white cross of France. In the chaotic hack and crush of a medieval battlefield anyone without clearly visible identification invited death from both sides, and badges - at the least, cheap cloth cut-outs of a lord's badge - were very widely worn.

Civilians too wore these emblems. Henry V of England required all Normans to wear the cross of St.George. In 1382 King Charles VI of France led an expedition into Flanders, and "there was not a man or woman in the country up to Ghent who did not wear a white cross". In 1411 the Parisians under Burgundian dominance wore blue hoods with a St.Andrew's cross and a shield-shape with a fleur-de-lys. A miniature in the Grimani Breviary shows a large Burgundian cross-and-firesteel badge roughly chalked or painted on a farmhouse wall beside the door.

Switzerland
In 1291 the three cantons of Uri, Schwyz and Unterwalden - hardy mountain folk, who fiercely resisted pressure from their Hapsburg masters - signed a treaty to support one another in time of need. In time other German-speaking territories and cities joined them to form, by the 15th century, a loose Confederation which would finally become modern Switzerland. Always fighting amongst themselves, but usually uniting in the face of outside threat, they were not considered a serious political power until the late 15th century. The city of Berne steadily increased its territory and rose to be the most powerful of the Confederation. A number of other Swiss cities could also field well-equipped contingents built around the bourgeoisie and guilds, sometimes employing mercenaries, and backed by the country folk in time of war. In 1475 they ravaged Savoyard territory, now the canton of Vaud, during a campaign of expansion; and when the "invincible" Burgundian army came to the aid of their Savoyard allies in 1476 the Swiss tumbled

them back in ruins at the battles of Murten and Grandson, capturing a booty so vast that it affected their economy. Suddenly a power to be reckoned with, Switzerland came blazing onto the European political and military scene.

Most Swiss, although subjects of the Empire, probably thought of themselves as Bernese, Lucerners, etc.; contemporary writers often referred to them as "Germans", and their armies frequently included soldiers from southern Germany and Alsace.

The bases of their strength were the *Knabenschaften,* young men's societies grouped according to parish, valley, town, or city guild. These tough, unruly 14 to 20-year-olds were considered the most expendable troops, usually forming the vanguard *(Vorhut)* in battle. The main body *(Gewalthaufen)* was mostly composed of older, steadier, better-equipped married men, forming the great pike blocks; a rearguard *(Nachhut)* formed the reserve. Ideally the three bodies moved in echelon, and they were capable of swift changes of direction in battle.

A selective form of conscription distinguished between the *Auszug,* young and mostly unmarried

(Left & below) Swiss pikemen typically dressed for a winter campaign: helmets and breast plates (one covered by a long gown), with long swords. One trails his pike as he walks, a practical way of marching with a long, vibrating shaft. Long hair was typical of Swiss and southern Germans in the late 1470s-80s, and beards seem to have been more common than supposed. *(Photos John Howe)*

(Right) French footsoldiers, two wearing the white cross on a red livery jacket or *paletot*. A variety of polearms were carried; halbards were first made in France in the 1470s by order of Louis XI, and the Curé St.Michael wrote that these "hallebardes" were "new equipment of war". *(Photo John Howe)*

(Below right) Officer of French infantry, c.1460; he wears light blue and red livery over a mailshirt, and the cross of France on his breast. His deep sallet is Italian in style but made by a one of the many armourers working in France. *(Photo Gerry Embleton)*

men; the *Landwehr*, older but active men, mostly married; and the *Landsturm*, only called out in time of emergency. All had to supply their own arms and equipment and report with food for a set period.

The soldiers were organised in groups of ten men (the *Rotte*, led by a *Rottenmeister*); between five and 20 *Rotten*, usually from the same or neighbouring parishes or guilds, formed a *Fähnlein*; and numbers of these formed the *Banner*, the guild or canton contingent, commanded by the *Oberster Feldhauptmann*. Each *Banner* had a staff including a scribe, surgeon, armourer, etc., and a standard-bearer with a bodyguard. This was an ideal; in practice each canton's force varied. Small contingents often brought their own priests, cooks, supporting craftsmen, etc.

Although an overall commander was elected for some campaigns, the rivalries and self-interest of the different contingents always worked against a centralised command. The control of the army was usually in the hands of what one modern historian has called "a council of sergeant-majors",

administering rules of conduct drawn up before each campaign by their city councils.

Livery

The Confederates wore a white cross usually on breast or back, left thigh, shoulder or hat. Some wore clothing in their city or cantonal colours, e.g. yellow and black for Uri; red and white for Schwyz, Soleur, Unterwalden and Thun; blue and white for Lucerne. These costumes were usually confined to musicians, standard-bearers, officers, and on occasion, cantinières. There are records of some whole contingents wearing the same colours - at the battle of Grandson the troops from St.Gallen were all in red with white crosses on their breasts - but it never seems to have been a widespread custom; most Swiss answered the call to arms in their everyday clothing.

Philippe de Commynes wrote of them after Grandson that "...they have become so accustomed to money, of which they had little experience previously...that they have come very near to falling out among themselves.Otherwise one would not know how to harm them,

for their lands are so rugged and poor and they are such good fighters that few men have tried to attack them...."

A 15th century guide to Europe observed of them that "...these men are cruel and rough people and fight all their neighbours if they ask for anything...."

Duke Charles wrote to the

Milanese ambassador Panagirola that "against the Swiss it will never do to march unprepared."

France

France in the 15th century was not one nation as we understand the term today. She was (as she still is) a country of vast regional differences, and it would be generations before one could truly speak of a French national army.

The defeats of Poitiers, Crécy and Agincourt shook France to the core and left England master of two-fifths of the present-day national territory, enjoying the allegiance of many French-speaking people. Although the Hundred Years' War united many French nobles in the common struggle against the English it nearly destroyed the Valois monarchy. The terrible war years emptied the coffers, and the ineffectual monarchy was completely at the mercy of the constantly quarrelling royal dukes. A miracle was needed – and appeared: Joan the Maid put new heart into the French soldiers. Crowned legitimately in Rheims cathedral in 1422, the weak Charles VII gradually acquired more power. Good generalship turned enthusiasm into victory, leading finally to the expulsion of the English.

The forces of the royal dukes – Berry, Anjou, Orleans and Burgundy – were the true sources

of power; and "French" military policy was shaped at any given moment by their never-ending manoeuvres for dominance and their shifting alliances. The Dukes of Burgundy emerged as the most powerful, allying themselves to the English and seeking a separate monarchy of their own.

In 1445 King Charles VII set in motion reforms which would eventually bring stability to his realm and power back to the hands of the monarchy. Armies had been raised in much the same way as in other European countries, based on the old feudal system. Various experiments had been attempted with permanent companies; and in 1446, with strong support from a war-weary populace, the king created the *compagnies d'ordonnance* – 20 companies each of 100 "lances" of six men. One source describes the lance as consisting of a man-at-arms in full armour; two archers wearing "leg armour, sallets, heavy jacks lined with linen or brigandines, bow in hand and quiver at side"; an attendant, a squire and a page.

The companies were assigned to different garrisons, paid out of special taxes, and each supported by its own bureaucracy. They

(Left) A French archer from the ancient cathedral city of Le Puy-en-Velay wears the city's yellow and blue on his helmet. His arrows are carried in a bag hanging from his shoulder, with his linen bow bag. France recruited many archers, and they were also seen in Germany and Switzerland, though the crossbow was always far more popular there. In eastern Europe and Italy a short "Turkish" bow was popular, although illustrations show the familiar so-called longbow in use. One northern Italian source shows two bows painted with intricate designs; and at least one southern German painting shows perfect examples of the great yew bows beloved of the English - hardly surprising, since some of England's yew staves were supplied from the region of Basle.

Spain and Portugal

The Iberian Peninsula, heavily influenced by its long Muslim occupation and hit hard by the Black Death, emerged after 300 years of warfare as a powerful Christian kingdom finally united under Isabella of Castile and her husband Fernando of Aragon. Wars between rival monarchs and crusades against the Moors attracted mercenaries from England, France and Germany, and occupied the energies of otherwise dangerously unemployed soldiers after the Hundred Years' War ended in the 1450s. Many took part in the final *reconquista* which ended with the fall of Grenada in 1492.

By the beginning of the 15th century the Peninsula monarchs were much influenced by their northern

were initially envisaged as a short-term measure to absorb the best of the thousands of ex-soldiers who had turned to banditry, and to be used to control the rest, who were "encouraged" to serve abroad. The idea of a "standing army" to restore order was popular; the taxes to pay for it were not. Many towns squirmed under the burden, trying to get their garrisons reduced or transferred; thousands sought exemption from the new tax, some merchants even joining the *compagnies d'ordonnana* in order to avoid helping pay for them!

Some companies behaved like the worst sort of occupying army, and there were violent episodes; but discipline slowly improved, a sort of esprit de corps was bom, and the king's control over his realm improved. By 1457 they were thought too valuable at home to be sent abroad to help the Scots against the English. The dangers of this state gendarmerie were recognised: de Commynes commented that "they brought security and peace to France, purchased at a great cost to the people..."

The Duke of Berry followed the king's example, and formed six permanent companies of 200 men-at-arms and 400 archers. In 1448, in an attempt to match the English archers, the king decreed that each parish would support one archer; exempt from certain taxes, he was to hold himself ready to serve when called. In Charles VII's reign (1422-61) there were 16 companies of about 500 archers each, increased to

a total of some 14,000 by Louis XI (1461-83). They seem never to have been a great success, however.

Livery

The king also had his personal guard, including the archers of the Compte de Clermont in red "cotte" and of the Compte d'Anjou in yellow, and the cavalry of the guard in red with a golden sun badge. His Scottish archer bodyguard were guardians of the royal standard; raised early in the century, they were reorganised in 1445. They had "...haquetons without sleeves of red, white and green [the king's personal livery] all charged with gold, having feathers in their sallets of the same colours, and their swords and leg armour richly adorned with silver...." They are shown in a contemporary illustration by Fouquet, all uniform in appearance, with armoured arms, legs and feet and short sleeves of brigandine work, armed with glaives or bows and bucklers.

French troops usually wore the white cross on breast and back; there are many references to livery colours being worn, and some to badges. In 1340 Tournail had sent 2,000 well-armed infantry to serve Philip of Valois "all clothed identically. Men from Dijon and Caen wore the name of their town, Metz and Lyon the arms of theirs." In 1477 Valenciennes "maintained at its own expense 150 German and Swiss handgunners who wore the livery and uniform of the town."

neighbours. The military terminology in use was Anglo-French; and in 1385 Juan I issued an ordinance of arms like those of France and England. Able-bodied men between 20 and 60 years of age could be called out for service, their equipment depending upon their income.

The great lords and bishops fielded considerable forces. There were large numbers of men-at-arms and light horse; foreign mercenaries were hired, and bodyguards formed a permanent foundation for the various royal and noble armies. The countryside and towns provided a militia of varying effectiveness. Moors, too, fought in the Spanish armies, though only against other Christians; in 1463 Henry IV of Castile had a Moorish guard.

Italy
Medieval Italy was torn by constant warfare between the many city states, and suffered particularly cruelly from recurring epidemics of the plague. Profiting from trade routes linking the Orient with the north, Italy boasted the largest cities in Europe (15th century Venice had some 100,000 inhabitants), and some of its most dazzling displays of wealth and culture - marred by regions of abject poverty, and a chaotic and ruthless political culture.

The various states organised their forces along roughly similar lines. Communal militias were slowly replaced by hired troops, or transformed into permanent paid units like those of Milan and Venice. *Condotta,* or contracts, were made with various *condottieri* to raise troops for specific campaigns. Successful *condottieri* hired smaller companies to make up the necessary forces: in 1441 Micheletto Attendolo, in the pay of Venice, recruited 167 *condottieri* each with between one and 50 "lances" , assembling an army of 561 lances.

Some *condottieri* rose to positions of great power. Muzio Attendolo was nicknamed Sforza - "force"; his son became Duke of Milan in 1450 as Francesco Sforza. These mercenary-lords sometimes intermarried, their families forming a kind of shadow aristocracy. Many were sought out by foreign paymasters; the Duke of Burgundy employed several - in 1472-73 their men contributed some 650 four-horse lances, 500 foot and 500 mounted crossbowmen to his army.

(Left) A Gascon soldier in the employ of the King of Aragon. He wean a gown over his breast plate and armour, and a hood under his sallet. A veteran professional soldier, he seeks employment further south now that the war with the English is over at last - his sort are not so welcome in France, but war is the only business he knows. *(Photo Gerry Embleton)*

(Right) An Italian mercenary officer and one of his company in the pay of Burgundy, lightly equipped for the long march through Savoy; he wears a sallet decorated with plume and padded roll in the colours of his company, and his town badge on his jack. Italian troops seem frequently to have worn the colours and badges of their towns or commanders, on clothing and sometimes on round or oval shields. *(Photo John Howe)*

England

King Henry V followed his great victory at Agincourt in 1415 with the conquest of Normandy in 1417-18. The year 1420 saw Henry married to the daughter of King Charles VI and recognised as heir to the French throne. England seemed unbeatable, her archers the masters of any battlefield.

Yet by 1422 Henry was dead of dysentery in a siege camp; and seven years later the 17-year-old mystic Jeanne d'Arc inspired a revival of French morale which long survived her judicial murder, the French working patiently towards final victory in the 1450s.

In the middle years of the century, all realistic hope of ruling France now lost, the warlike English turned inwards on themselves. The country was torn apart by bitter rivalry between the royal houses of York and Lancaster; for 30 years until 1485 the nobility of England fought against each other in the bloody series of civil wars now known as the Wars of the Roses.

By the 14th century the system of calling men up by "commission of array" - with all men obliged to serve, armed according to their income - had fallen into decay. English armies of the 15th century were raised through a series of contracts between the king and major military leaders; each commander was responsible for paying his troops, the king agreeing to repay the money at a later date.

As in continental countries, there was usually a royal guard, often of archers; the "lance" was used as the unit of administration; and detailed ordinances were frequently drawn up, covering the hundreds of different details necessary to the organisation of an army.

As one of the great military powers, England and her soldiers attracted considerable attention; and observers clearly found certain other characteristics of the island race as striking as their prowess in battle.

In 1486, during the "crusade" against the Moors in Spain, a Spanish chronicler described English veterans of the Wars of the Roses serving under Earl Rivers, "... men who had been hardened in certain civil wars which had raged in their country. They were huge feeders and deep carousers, often unruly and noisy in their wassail. Though from a remote and somewhat barbarous island they yet believe themselves to be the most perfect men on earth."

A secretary wrote in 1498, for the information of Andrea Trevisano, the Venetian ambassador to England: "The English are great lovers of themselves, and of everything belonging to them. They think that there are no other men than themselves and no other world but England, and whenever they see a handsome foreigner they say that 'he looks like an Englishman'....

"Although they all attend Mass every day and say many Paternosters in public...they always hear Mass on Sunday in their parish church, and give liberal alms...

"They have a very high reputation in arms; and from the great fear the French entertain of them, one must believe it to be justly acquired. But I have it on the best information that when the war is raging most furiously they will seek for good eating, and all their other comforts, without thinking what harm might befall them."

(Photo: below Gerry Embleton, right Alan & Michael Perry)

The Empire

The Holy Roman Empire consisted of interrelated but more or less independent duchies, counties and cities in Germany itself; and the lands of the three powerful families which had at different times supplied the Emperor - Austria, the Tyrol, Styria and other Hapsburg territories; the Rhineland, Bavaria, Holland and Friesia, lands of the Wittelsbachs; and the Luxembourg territories including Bohemia, Moravia and Silesia.

Frederick III (1440-93), King and Emperor, Hapsburg and Austrian, had neither the power nor the financial resources to hold together his sprawling domains. His position was always weakened by the fact that he was voted to his throne by seven powerful regional magnates - "electors" - each intent on preserving his own autonomy and on limiting Imperial control. The Emperor's plans to raise troops required the approval of the Imperial Diet (parliament) - which was usually slow in coming, and granted less than he asked for.

The eastern territories were threatened by the Turks, and border wars were always flaring up; in the west the ever-growing power of Burgundy nibbled at the Empire. The long term effects of these twin threats would in fact prove beneficial: the Empire rallied and strengthened to fill the vacuum left by the fall of the house of Burgundy in 1477. Marriage made the young Emperor Maximilian ruler of the rich Netherlands, and in the 16th century the Empire grew in strength and vitality under the Hapsburg dynasty.

Recruiting the peasants under the old feudal system was thought dangerous by a nobility always fearful of insurrection, and money was increasingly found to hire mercenaries; towns, too, began to pay professionals. There were so many knights, bishops, towns and cities struggling for their rights, constantly at odds with one another and with the peasantry, that the Empire can hardly ever be described as united.

The rates of pay for the different types of soldiers changed little between Crécy in 1347 and Edward IV's French expedition of 1475; and various inducements had to be offered to secure recruits. In troubled times the troops of some powerful noblemen were under arms so often that they took on the character of private armies. In return for service the soldiers annually received "livery" - food, clothes, lodgings and pay; wearing their lord's colours and badges, they supported him in his quarrels great and small. When the Hundred Years' War finally dragged to its inglorious conclusion in 1453-57, many unemployed soldiers swelled the ranks of the nobles' retinues.

John Howard, Duke of Norfolk wrote to John Paston before Bosworth: "I pray you bring such a company of tall men as you may, and ordain them jackets of my livery". In June 1499 the Duke of Norfolk and 200 men dressed in his livery of blue and tawny accompanied the king during a visit to that county, "...the blewe on the leffte syde, and both dark colors".

In 1470 a levy from Canterbury joined the Calais garrison; they were supplied with "jackettes" of red cloth, bearing white roses of "karsay" as badges. In 1461 a contingent to the garrison from Rye also wore red. The Duke of Warwick was Captain of Calais; his men wore red jackets embroidered before and behind with his ragged staff badge. We do not know if the men from Canterbury and Rye wore red because it was their own colour, Warwick's livery, or simply a common colour for soldiers.

Two ballads describe Sir William Stanley's men wearing coats "...as red as any blood", with his hart's head badge; and "jackettes that were of white and red".

At times soldiers might wear the badges both of their own lord and of their overall commander. At the second battle of St.Albans in 1461 men of the Lancastrian army wore their "lordys leverey that every man myghte know his own feleschippe by hys leverey", and every man also bore the badge of Prince Edward, son of Henry VI - a bend of crimson and black with ostrich feathers.

(Right) A soldier of the town militia of Ravensburg in Westphalia waits in the dawn street for his company to muster; his town colours are displayed on his hood, a common place for insignia. The company's armour is packed in wagons; he will march in warm, comfortable clothes, lightly armed with helmet and halbard, carrying his belongings in a sack and with cold rations for the first day's march in his haversack.
(Photo Gerry Embleton)

Army organisation roughly followed other European models. The German equivalent of the "lance" was the *Gleven,* usually comprising a man-at-arms, a page, up to three mounted archers or crossbowmen, and perhaps two servants. Town militia forces varied, and often included hired mercenaries - in fairly small contingents, given the expense. Many towns had a drill and muster place, set up shooting grounds, and accumulated impressive arsenals of handguns and artillery.

An example of the structure of a typical town contingent comes from surviving documents describing Frankfurt troops who went to join the Imperial army in 1477. A *Hauptmann* (captain) led 197 *Fussknechte* (footsoldiers) and 26 *Reisige* (mounted men-at-arms), uniformly dressed and equipped, with a red and white banner, wagons, wagoners, cooks, craftsmen and a priest. The foot were divided into eight *Rotten,* each comanded by a a *Rotten-meister* (equivalent to a modern NCO) responsible for its welfare and discipline.

The Emperor's badge of a black eagle on yellow was worn by officials and on the banners, wagons and tents of an Imperial army; many town and regional contingents wore their own livery; sometimes both were displayed together. There are examples of completely uniform dress, if not arms and equipment; and of wagons being uniformly painted.

In 1474 the Bishop of Munster led a large force of horse and foot "all clothed in green" to the relief of the siege of Neuss. Lubeck troops wore red and white; Frankfurt troops were issued with two *ellen* of brown and red cloth to make hose and hoods, and received one gulder each to buy jackets. At the siege of Hericourt in 1474 Strasbourg troops wore half-red, half-white clothes; those from Colmar, red and blue; Villigen, white and blue; Walshut and the Black Forest, all black; Lindow, white and green. In honour of their Swiss allies they all wore white crosses.

(Right) A soldier of the Duke of Thierstein's household stands sentry on the gates of the castle of Haute-Koenigsbourg in Alsace - part of the duke's reward for turning against the Duke of Burgundy at Nancy in 1477. *(Photo Gerry Embleton)*

(Below) A German *Hauptmann* has placed his sentries and makes his rounds. His company are fortunate, billeted at a prosperous monastery; the captain will dine excellently with the abbot tonight, and his men, welcome as protectors against troublesome peasants, will be well fed. The captain wears a gown over his armour, and a typically German kettle hat with a mail aventail; he carries a mace. The sentry is well armed and armoured, and carries a distinctively German style of halbard. *(Photo Gerry Embleton)*

Burgundy

Wrote John Paston in 1468: "As for the dukes court I heard never of none like to it, save king Arthurs court."

By a mixture of political cunning, strategic marriage, ruthless conquest and considerable luck, the four generations of 15th century Burgundian dukes (Frenchmen, of the royal house of Valois) dominated a slowly coalescing mass of small but important territories and towns. Their fluctuating power over the French court brought them immense prestige and frequent showers of gold; but their lands were frustratingly divided - in the north, Flanders, the Low Countries and part of France, and further south the duchy and county of Burgundy with its capital at Dijon, the two linked by a broken chain of smaller possessions. It was ever the dukes' desire to consolidate this dispersed realm; and the last of them, Charles the Bold, had ambitions to be crowned a king in his own right by the Emperor.

The Burgundian Netherlands sat astride some of the most important trade routes in Europe, and ample waterways and roads linked its ports with the granaries of Artois and Hainault, the ore-producing Ardennes, the immense resources and markets along the Rhine, and the land

routes to Italy, gateway to the Orient. Burgundy's harbours were open to the great spider-web of Hanseatic ports, to Prussia's grain, the timbers and furs of the Baltic, even to the gates of Muscovy. From Spain, Italy and the Levant wine, fruit, silk, spices - the whole Mediterranean trade from the East - flowed up through the passes and on to Burgundy's court, the richest in northern Europe.

Van Eyck and Van der Weyden painted for Burgundy's nobles and wealthy merchants; the greatest masters of European music composed for them; Burgundian fashions were jealously copied. Philippe de Commynes (1447-1511) wrote that "the subjects of the house of Burgundy lived in great wealth because of peace and the goodness of their prince who did not burden them with heavy taxes". Flattering words; but research has shown that - despite the inevitable social inequalities - the Burgundian Netherlands did enjoy golden years between 1440 and 1470.

The Burgundians never wholly subdued their realm. Their cities, like those all over Europe, were growing richer and stronger, and as they increased in size and prestige (Bruges was bigger than London) they chafed under the old rules, demanding greater independence. The dukes did not balk at seducing their subjects with

Uniforms

John the Fearless, Duke of Burgundy (r. 1404–19) adopted as a badge a carpenter's plane - a punning reference to his intention of "smoothing" the wooden club badge of his arch-enemy the Duke of Orleans. He used this badge profusely, giving away hundreds in gold and silver to gentlemen and servants. It embellished his armour, and adorned 3,000 scarlet pennons for his troops, the coloured cloth powdered with "flying wood shavings".

This symbol evolved into the similarly shaped firesteel, flint and flying sparks used as a badge by his grandson Charles the Bold (r.1467-77). Charles's ordinances laid down that of the troops under his direct command each man-at-arms must have blue and white plumes in his sallet and a vermilion St.Andrew's cross for his armour; and that archers and others should have a blue and white *paletot* or livery jacket bearing a red St.Andrew's cross.

Other companies of the Burgundian army probably wore the colours of their *conducteurs* - the high nobility of the Burgundian state such as Luxembourg, St.Pol, Croy, and their captains. The wearing of blue and white may have become more widespread, as we read that Burgundian reinforcements for Nancy in 1477, led by Philippe de Croy, consisted of 800 infantry "in blue and white, with two months' pay in their pouches". *(Photo left: Gary Embleton)*

Savoy

The territory of Savoy lay to the south and west of the Swiss Confederation, reaching the Jura and Lake Neuchâtel, north-west to the Saône, south to Turin and Nice. Louis XI of France, the Duke of Burgundy, the powerful city of Berne and the Duke of Milan all had their eyes on Savoyard territory, but Savoy survived between these balanced threats. In 1472-75 Burgundian influence became stronger when Duke Charles and Yolande, Duchess and Regent of Savoy allied themselves more closely. Charles took into his service Jacques de Romont, Baron of Vaud, and thus controlled a major trade route between Germany and the south. His Italian mercenaries began to cross Vaud en route from Italy to Burgundy; Berne objected, savagely raiding and effectively capturing Vaud - and thus provoking the Burgundian wars, with unforeseen consequences.

(Below) 1475: two Savoyard soldiers of the garrison of Chillon on Lake Geneva, wearing Savoy's red livery and white cross. One has a very up-to-date handgun and a pewter powder flask. Parti-coloured hose and helmets imported from Milan betray a slight Italian influence.
(Photo John Howe)

soft words, or frightening them with growls of warning, into paying more taxes or providing military support; but if rebellion went too far they could be as savagely brutal as any medieval monarch. When Charles the Bold's army was beaten by the Swiss at Murten and Grandson in 1476 many, nursing old grievances, turned against him; and when he was finally hacked to death in the snow at Nancy the following year his glittering dukedom was soon parcelled out among his old enemies.

Burgundian armies

Until 1471 the ducal armies consisted of the household guards of the duke, the nobles and their retainers, the town militias, and mercenaries. The armoured men-at-arms formed the powerful nucleus, supported by numerous mounted archers, crossbowmen, swordsmen, etc.; a smaller number of infantry; and a large supporting force, organised with bureaucratic thoroughness, of artillery, engineers, transport, and countless craftsmen.

Raising troops and hiring mercenaries anew for each campaign was too slow for Duke Charles; his ambitions demanded a powerful standing army, and in 1467 he started to pay soldiers to stay under arms after a campaign. In April 1471 he began recruiting for permanent companies inspired by the French *compagnies d'ordonnance*. Between 1471 and 1473 the warlike young duke organised a powerful standing army, detailing in a series of meticulous ordinances the exact organisation, conduct, arms, equipment, and livery of each class of soldiery - in peace, in war, in billets, on the march, and in battle. Remarkably, his ordinances survive; but it may be that such meticulous "king's regulations" were in common use throughout the medieval period.

Organisation varied but was generally built around the "lance": a man-at-arms and his followers (in 1473, three archers, a swordsman, a crossbowman, a handgunner, a pikeman and a servant). Six lances formed a *chambre*, 25 lances a squadron, four squadrons a company (though few units were usually up to their "paper" strength). A carefully regulated system of flags and pennons identified each unit.

CAMPAIGN LIFE

(Right) Swiss troops on the way to raise the siege of Grandson, March 1476; in spite of bad weather they made good time from Berne - at the end march discipline broke down as each contingent strove to arrive before their rivals. Before the battle of Murten that June 2,500 men from Zurich marched 140km (87 miles) to Berne in three days, though they left hundreds of stragglers along the route. After resting for a few hours they marched on to Murten and into battle. *(Photo Carlos Oliveira)*

(Below) Burgundian pikemen on the march in hostile territory, fully armed and watchful. *(Photo John Howe)*

It is difficult to assess the state of medieval roads, and impossible to generalise. Clearly their condition presented no major obstacle to military or commercial movements. Various regulations for their care existed; in England each landowner was responsible for a stretch of road, and was required to clear the undergrowth for 200 yards on each side to deter lurking robbers. It was important that trade and express courier routes, and roads linking castles and other strategically important points should function properly; they were the arteries through which the lifeblood of commerce flowed, and there is no reason to suppose that they were normally neglected.

Logistics

No medieval soldiers simply leapt into the saddle, waved their swords and galloped out of a castle to go on campaign. When a large medieval army went to war it faced the same logistical problems as any other before the invention of motorised transport. Wherever relevant documents survive - and many do - they prove this to be so.

Basic food and drink for several days, or even weeks, had to be carried on pack animals, or in wagons and carts pulled by horses or oxen - which also had to be fed. Arrows and bolts in their hundreds of thousands, spare bows and strings, artillery, powder and shot, armourers and their equipment, tents and camping kit, tools of all kinds, materials for sieges and bridge-building, clothing, bedding, medical supplies, the personal gear of the officers' establishments...ton upon ton of impedimenta had to be transported, much of it packed in (sometimes padlocked) barrels.

The wagons and draught animals in turn needed more wagons for fodder, tools, forges, smiths, wheelwrights, and farriers. Transport had to be provided for all the men who kept the transport rolling; for those who pitched and struck the camp, and kept the barrels and bales packed securely and properly loaded; and for the clerks and quartermasters who noted, stored and issued it all, and made sure it arrived in the right place at the right time. Wagons and drivers were sometimes on the military establishment, but were more often civilian, hired or pressed at need. We read of 500 wagons collected for carrying food to King Edward's army in 1481; and small detachments often had

their own wagons.

A German source from the end of the century lists the number of wagons needed by an army on the march: for 12,000 people on foot, 650 wagons; for 3,000 cavalry, 300 wagons. With such a force of infantry marching three abreast; 3,000 horse riding by twos; and allowing 10m. between each of the 950 wagons (since heavy loads needed teams of six to eight animals), this gives our army a total length on the march of 23km-say 14 miles; and if they all camped together it would be several hours into the day before the rear of the column could set off, by which time the head of the column would be well on their way towards the next night's bivouac.

The speed of march naturally depended on the condition of the roads, the season and weather; but armies were occasionally capable of moving surprisingly fast, which argues for good organisation and well maintained roads.

The Black Prince's great raid from Bordeaux to the Channel coast and back in October/ November 1355 averaged 15km (more than 9 miles) daily for 900km (560 miles): impressive, for an army which assaulted many towns en route, and was laden with booty. Research indicates that crusading armies covered a daily average of between 10km and 16km (6.2 to 10 miles) on very long marches. Today a steady walking pace over reasonable paths is reckoned at 4km an hour, 20 to 30km a day (12 to 18 miles) for a single person - the larger the group the slower the progress; but military emergency can produce multiples of this figure.

(Photo above: Alan & Michael Perry)

In contrast to the speed of marching armies, official and commercial courier services - using relays of riders and horses - were common in the 15th century, and could achieve remarkable speeds. In 1406 a diplomat travelled from London to Milan - 600 miles, across the Channel and the Alps - in six days. By the end of the century royal post services were averaging 80-95 miles (128- 152km) a day in summer, 60-80 (96-128km) in winter.

In the 14th century the Venetian Republic maintained a regular courier service between Venice and Bruges, taking seven days - compared with the several weeks a normal traveller might spend on the journey. A merchant with pack horses or a small party of mounted men might average 25 miles (40km) a day; 33 miles (53km) was considered a forced pace, impossible to keep up for more than a day or two. A lone traveller might manage that figure, or 50 miles (80km) with changes of horses. The Duke of Burgundy, a spectacular traveller who changed his residence 100 times in one year, averaged 37 miles (59km) a day for more than five days, with an escort of 30 knights.

(Below left) Soldiers would not march in their armour if they could help it; this footsoldier has put his brigandine on the baggage wagon. He wears hat and gown, and carries rations and a blanket-roll. *(Photo Gerry Embleton)*

(Below) March 1461: John Paston described parties of Norfolk levies on their way to London to join their king as "straggling about by themselves". Without good organisation and leadership soldiers leaving their own familiar countryside could easily get lost, in an age before signposted roads and reliable maps. *(Photo Gerry Embleton)*

(Right & below right) Weary troops rest in the late summer sun. No canteens were issued but we can be sure many carried them, or were supplied with drink by their womenfolk on the march. Even in "civilised" Europe an army in unfamiliar terrain might be without a water supply for a day or two, and in hard times stragglers could expect no mercy from the peasantry. *(Photos Philippe Krauer/ L'Illustré; John Howe)*

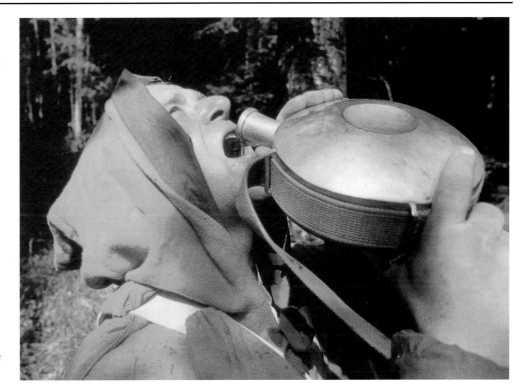

Music and Pastimes

We know almost nothing about 15th century military music. One or two pieces survive which may have been played as marches, and some secular songs - though mostly in versions written later - which could have been popular with soldiers. There may be echoes of a medieval sound in the traditional drumming techniques which are still practised in Basle, though much changed over the centuries. Troops had begun to march in step to the rhythm of drums, and of fifes, shawms and bagpipes; all the Swiss chronicles show fife, small drum and bagpipes played by armed musicians marching at the heads of columns - but we can only guess at what sounds they made. Trumpets, horns and drums were used for signalling and, with other instruments, to entertain or impress.

The soldiers no doubt sang - and their songs were no doubt the inevitable and timeless mixture of religion, sentiment and bawdy. In some ways soldiers never change: Philippe de Commynes described English troops in 1475, "some singing, some were asleep, and all were drunk..."; and a Burgundian soldier marching on his way might have sung these words:

"Adieu ces bans vins de Lannoys,
Adieu dames, adieu borgois,
Adieu celle que tant amoye,
Adieu toute playssante joye..."

("Farewell to the good wines of Lannoys/ Farewell to the ladies and gentlemen/ Farewell to the girl I love so much/ Farewell to all pleasant joys...")

(Below) English soldiers amuse themselves with the warrior's ancient pastime - dice. In the 15th century cards, bowls, ball games, board games, and many children's group games that today would be considered too simple for adults - though played then rather more robustly - helped the soldier pass the long days of boredom. *(Photos Carlos Oliveira; Alan & Michael Perry)*

(Right) The St.Gallen contingent that set out, 440 strong, to join the Confederate army in the relief of the siege of Murten in 1476 took two carts each pulled by five horses. One was loaded with provisions including eight sides of bacon, dried beef, two sacks of salt, barley, oatmeal and butter; the second, with cooking pots, kettles with hooks and tripods, 52 dishes, scythes, sickles and other tools. They had their own cook, chaplain, and 300 gulden for pay. Clearly they were equipped to cater for themselves perfectly adequately. *(Photo John Howe)*

Tents and Camps

When a prince or duke went to war he tried to take with him as much of the comfort and richness of his home as was practical, and to keep up his accustomed display of wealth and ceremony. Many-roomed tents of satin and brocade, thickly carpeted and hung with rich tapestries, housed the lord and his retinue. We have very detailed descriptions of Burgundian and Imperial camps, as well as that of Henry VIII in France in 1513, and there is no reason to suppose that other kings and great nobles settled for less. The establishments of lesser lords and knights were relatively smaller and simpler, but they too had their retinues, and love of display extended throughout the propertied classes.

Duke Philip the Good's tent in the camp at Boulogne was "of extraordinary size, larger than ever seen before. The construction was so vast and elegant as to capture all eyes. It was a pavilion in the form of a town surrounded by wooden towers and crenellated walls. The entrance consisted of two great towers with a curtain suspended in between. In the middle of the tent was the main room, from which extended, like the spokes of a wheel, a large number of apartments separated by tiny alleys, in which *it was said* [our italics] that 3,000 people could be lodged." This portable palace contained many dining rooms, bedrooms and a chapel.

Both Charles the Bold and Henry VIII took prefabricated wooden houses on campaign; Charles set his up between two great pavilions in which he took his meals and held council. The fabric of the tents captured by the Swiss at Grandson was rich enough to be cut up for church vestments; after the battle there must have been many a wooden house in the Alpine valleys boasting bed-covers and cushions fit for a lord.

(Below) Handgunners come back from picket duty protecting the Burgundian camp near Lausanne, 1476. Planks have been laid as pathways through the mud by the "men of the camp"; and this company, like many others, has set up its own kitchen tents.
(Photo John Howe)

Most of the Burgundian officers, and many soldiers, were also provided with tents or billeted in farms and villages. In Henry VIII's English army it was forbidden to provide tents for the troops on the grounds that they took up too much wagon-space and too much time, but many captains provided them nonetheless. A contemporary document in the Lille archives describes tents for the Burgundian army; tents and camp equipment were considered important, and ate up one-fifth of the Receiver of Artillery's total budget. In January 1476 the army received "600 small tents and pavilions, 100 other square pavilions, two wooden houses, 130 square tentelletes, 50 other pavilions, six large tents and six large square pavilions and another wooden house". A tent could be 24ft. by 30ft., a pavilion 11ft. to 13ft. in diameter, and the price of different models was between 4 and 8 livres. Frequent purchases of "canevas" are recorded, to make "273 pavilions, 100 stables etc.". We find mention of *bourgherain bleu,* a strong fabric used to line tents; and of ribbons, laces, fringes, rings and "hooked pegs". There was a special department to issue and repair tents, with its own carpenters, wagons, horses – and, of course, an accounts office.

Tents were decorated with identifying emblems, shields and flags, and appliqué strips of coloured cloth reinforcing the seams and making simple designs. One tent in the Schilling chronicles has a small written label beside the door – tantalisingly illegible.

Many camps were fortified, or surrounded by wagons mounting mantlets and guns. A German source shows wagons with tall wickerwork wagon-boxes filled with earth, and others supporting a wall of loopholed mantlets and breech-loading guns mounted behind sliding panels.

Camps could be enormous, laid out in streets by the pioneers with hundreds of tents, markets, horselines for thousands of animals, and an inner camp for the commanders. A site like this for 10,000 soldiers and their followers must have resembled a fair-sized, bustling town on market day.

(Left) The woman of an officer of a Swiss contingent packs her furniture for loading. The captured tent still bears the insignia of an Italian unit of Duke Charles's army; the long-legged chest-cum-table is typical – and on it, note her man's turban with ostrich plume and badge. She wears Swiss or south German headdress, and has taken off her sleeves to work. *(Photo Carlos Oliveira)*

Those without tents were more or less adept at making shelters from hay, branches or looted timber, and some probably carried canvas or blankets to make a "hale" or bivouac. In 1523 a Welsh soldier in France sneered at improvident campaigners: "...And yet they had no reason to complain except of their own sluggishness and slovenliness. For there was no lack of food and drink or wood for fire and making huts, and plenty of straw to roof them and to lie on if they only fetched it, but there were many a man weak in body who preferred from sheer laziness to lie under the hedge rather than take the trouble to make a snug warm hut...".

(Opposite top) *Jumpfern* - young unmarried girls - provided important support for the troops of what is now Switzerland and the surrounding areas, and no doubt for many other armies too. They were maids-of-all-work - cooking, foraging, washing and repairing, looking after animals - and were no doubt capable of looking after themselves, handling weapons and helping defend the camp if needed. There is mention of the Basle authorities paying two girls with cloth for their military service, and they appear in many illustrations of camp life. The meal this girl is cooking will feed heartily the 50-odd men of her company. *(Photo John Howe)*

(Left & below) Great military camps were like teeming cities, exciting places for a young recruit where anything and everything could be had at a price...but they had a darker side. If they occupied the same ground for any length of time they were notorious for breeding "camp fever" - typhoid or cholera - due to poor hygiene and sanitation and polluted water supplies. In the crowded camps disease spread like wildfire; as winter approached, life in some siege camps took on a nightmare quality. *(Photos Gerry Embleton)*

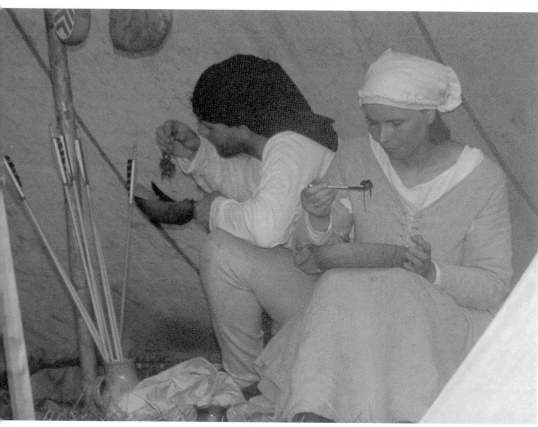

(Left) Inside their simple A-shaped tent a German archer and his wife eat the rations which she has purchased in the camp market, and cooked in the cauldrons she shares with a few comrades. *(Photo Carlos Oliveira)*

(Below) Soldiers might sleep crowded into barns and outhouses, spreading their bedrolls on the hay, like this English soldier of the 1460s. Accounts of British troops' experiences in such French and Belgian billets in the First World War strike a strong echo of the environment in which their ancestors must have lived 400 years before.

The Burgundian ordinances describe the drill to be followed on the morning of departure. Three trumpet calls were sounded: at the first, everyone had to pack his gear; at the second, the troops were to fall in with their various small units; at the third, these were to form up into the proper companies under their banners. *(Photo Robert Hoare)*

(Above & right) Troops were often billeted in farms, villages and town houses. The Burgundian ordinance of October 1473 lays down strict regulations. The soldiers are to wait in their ranks outside the village while an officer from each company inspects the available lodgings; once allocated billets they must not seek any other. If they are to stay for long they may choose between living in hostels or, with the householder's consent, in private dwellings. Officers are responsible for their men's good conduct; records are to be kept of any complaints, and damages paid for out of the culprit's wages. Food is to be paid for, and the common practice of forcing the host to buy wine for the soldiers is to stop....

Not all soldiers were brutes; and some, no doubt, found very cosy billets indeed.
(Photos Gerry Embleton; Philippe Krauer/ L'Illustré)

Feeding an army

To feed a medieval army was a colossal undertaking. When invading hostile territory commanders took into consideration whatever might be captured or harvested; and foraging expeditions on a large scale could devastate the countryside, using force on friend and foe alike. But even the most ruthless "scorchers" can only live off the land with difficulty if they descend in great numbers - an army needed food in industrial quantities.

Just how much they needed can be calculated from an example in the 15th century writings of Christine de Pisan. She listed the following provisions for a garrison of 600 men for six months:
60 tons of Paris wheat, one-third baked into biscuit, the rest to be ground into flour.
40 tons of beans, 2 tons of peas.
120 pipes of wine, 2 pipes of vinegar, 1 pipe oil.
1 ton of salt, 1 pipe salted butter, 10-12lbs of rice, 50lbs. of spices, ginger, pepper etc., 15lbs of almonds, 2lbs of saffron, 2 quarters mustard seed.
100 oxen live or salted, 100-120 fletches bacon, 160 sheep.
As much poultry "as men will", 1,000 eels (presumably smoked or dried), 25 barrels of herring.

Based on this, an army of 12,000 men in the field for a six-week campaign would need 300 tons of wheat, 200 tons of beans, 500 oxen, 500 fletches of bacon, 900 sheep, 600 pipes of wine, etc.

In 1420 the English garrison at Carentan in France consisted of two men-at-arms and 20 archers; a contemporary document records that their diet consisted of wheat, cider, salt, fish, eggs and cheese, and each month six beeves or cows, plus 22 sheep or seven sides of bacon, plus hay and oats for their animals. This seems a large amount for 22 men, and it may be that various servants and artisans were not listed as part of the garrison.

In 1431 during the war against the Hussites 78 men-at-arms and 284 soldiers left the city of Regensburg. They took with them a reserve of cereal for six weeks, 90 beeves, 90 quintels of dried meat, 9 quintels of lard, 1,200 cheeses, 80 dried cod, 56 livres of tallow candles, two large and 73 small barrels of Austrian wine, 138 small barrels of beer, plus vinegar, vegetable oil, pepper, saffron, ginger, etc.

Mills and bakers accompanied the armies. In "friendly" country an attempt was made to buy such supplies as were not carried, or concentrated in advance in magazines along the planned route. Regional produce affected the diet, but all the items in Christine de Pisan's list were common, as were every kind of salted, dried or smoked meat, fish and fowl. Fish are often listed - cod, skate, eels, pickled herring, Mediterranean pilchards; with eggs and cheese these replaced meat on fasting days, which seem to have been strictly observed by all levels of society. The diet was enlivened with raisins, dried apples and pears, onions, garlic, oil, wild and cultivated herbs, vegetables, salads, and practically anything else that grew, flew, ran or hopped.
(Photos below: Claude Huyghens & Françoise Danrigal, Hans Weber)

Soldiers' food

We do not know how or when rations were issued to 15th century soldiers in camp, and customs probably varied widely. We know that cooks sometimes accompanied a contingent. It appears that soldiers were issued their basic rations, and made their own arrangements for cooking just as they would until the late 19th century. Some documents speak of soldiers having to buy rations out of their pay.

Great markets were sometimes set up near encamped armies. At the siege of Neuss a huge market was laid out within the Burgundian camp, with streets for stallholders marked out with cords. Apothecaries, craftsmen, drapers, shoemakers, hatters, barbers, cutlers, lantern and candle makers all set up shop, alongside grocers, butchers, fishmongers and suppliers of hay and oats. Such organisation was only possible when camps settled in for a long time.

The basics - bread or biscuits, salt pork or beef, beans and cheese - would be familiar to any soldier down the centuries. As always, when the food was issued in reasonable condition it was as good or bad as the cook. Properly soaked salt pork, dried peas and fresh bread washed down with good ale or cider can make a delicious meal, which improves with every chance-picked or chance-snared addition. Ancient, half-cooked salt beef and weevil-infested "hard tack" eaten cold, on the march or in the rain, are as deadly to morale as the enemy's arrows.

The system of supply, and the financial structure that supported it, were fragile, and quickly broke down in the face of setbacks. A lost battle, a prolonged siege, a missed rendezvous or promised supplies witheld, and hunger joined disease and violent death to stalk the marching troops. Hungry soldiers are unscrupulous even in their own country, and the many mercenaries in 15th century armies lacked even the vague inhibition of common nationality.

The arrival of a large, hungry army - even a "friendly" one - in a rural area could be biblical in its consequences. If the winter store of harvested crops and seed grain were taken; the few cherished cattle kept alive for the spring run off; tools and carts stolen; fences and outbuildings torn apart for firewood - then winter brought famine to whole communities. Famine brought violent population shifts: the peasants who did not starve fled to the nearest towns; on their heels came disease, and the breakdown of order. The terror of plundering armies is one of the most ancient and universal of mankind's folk-memories.
(Photo Carlos Oliveira)

(Right) Like armies throughout history until the invention of canning, medieval soldiers took the campaign road with large droves of cattle on the hoof, to be slaughtered and butchered daily for fresh meat. These must have slowed down the march, and added to the congestion of the roads, the wear and tear on their fabric, the number of additional hands (and mouths) which had to follow the tail of the army, and the damage to the countryside. But while the campaign went well and the cattle lasted, at least the soldiers ate adequately.

Contemporary manuals set out ideal quantities for rations, which are corroborated by the financial accounts of actual deliveries. We can draw up a list of a "typical" day's rations for a well-fed 15th century soldier: 1.25-1.5kg of bread; a *pfund* or 468g of fresh meat; 6g salt pork; 7g eggs; 14g cheese; 13g butter - a total of about 4,300-4,500 calories a day, sufficient for hard physical work in the open air. To this might be added vegetables or fruit as available.
(Photo Anne Embleton)

Officers' food

There are many myths about medieval food. There is absolutely no evidence for large quantities of spices being used to disguise the taste of badly preserved foods; the medieval cook was perfectly capable of salting, smoking and drying meats and fish, and merchants selling rotten food could be prosecuted. Many recipes survive, mostly for elaborate dishes. (Attempts to recreate such dishes today are hampered by the absence of quantities in these recipes - common phrases are "the usual amount" or "a good amount".) Most gentlemen going on campaign would have taken their cooks with them, among their many servants. Princes and noblemen had camp kitchens set up to feed their considerable households, and these were also capable of serving banquets sufficiently elaborate to impress the guests and dignitaries who seem to have visited military camps in a steady stream. The menus might be influenced by the host's relative wealth and generosity, his curent tastes or his personal medical regime, ranging from robust simplicity to the dizzy peaks of culinary art.
(Photos: right Carlos Oliveira, below Philippe Krauer/ L'Illuré)

It is debatable to what extent hunting contributed to the soldier's table. Hunting of all kinds was a necessary and very popular aspect of medieval life, and the gentleman's favourite sport. Armies usually moved along roads and campaigned in cultivated areas around centres of population, where game would be relatively scarce – and anyway elusive, when disturbed by the passage of thousands of travelling soldiers. No doubt, if game was to be found within a day's ride of a medieval army, and if it were not too dangerous to hunt because of the presence of the enemy, then enthusiastic huntsmen would try their luck and skill.

(Photos Philippe Krauer/ L'Illustré)

Women

The concept of "equal rights" for women was totally foreign to the medieval world. Many women were virtual slaves to their parents or husbands, and we may say that for many life was restricted, narrow and menial. Yet there is also plentiful evidence that many others led reasonably rich and full lives, being at least as free as their husbands, and in some cases as free as they are today. Many entered the arts, crafts and business world, and prospered. We read of Rose of Burford, who became a member of the association of "merchants of the staple", exporting wool to Calais. Widowhood among the bourgeois class could bring the means and scope to exercise considerable independent power. One example, Agnes Fingerin of Gorlitz in Germany, survived her textile merchant husband by 50 years, ran a thriving business, and established a fund for poor relief-she was remembered until recent times for the annual distribution to the poor known as *Agnetenbrot* - "Agnes's bread".

The commonest way for a woman to enter what was usually a male-dominated commercial world was as helper to a husband or father, sometimes as an equal partner, taking over the daily conduct of affairs in his old age or carrying on his business after his death. This was particularly true of a craftsman's wife, who might run his shop and all trade affairs while he concentrated on production. Merchants might hand over whole sectors of their businesses to their womenfolk. We have records of many female shopkeepers, and of women working in almost every common trade: as butchers, bakers, candlestick makers, armourers, money-lenders, messengers, workers in metal, wood and textiles; as dealers in cloth, iron, arms, saddlery, coal, and spices.

In Cologne in 1468-69 female wine merchants controlled ten per cent of the trade; one woman controlled 24 per cent of the sugar market, another, nearly ten per cent of the lead imports; and these are not rare exceptions. Apprenticeships in the textile and clothing guilds were usually open to women; and within the guilds they could occasionally rise to become master craftsmen.

*(Photos above, above right:
Claude Huyghens & Françoise Danrigal)*

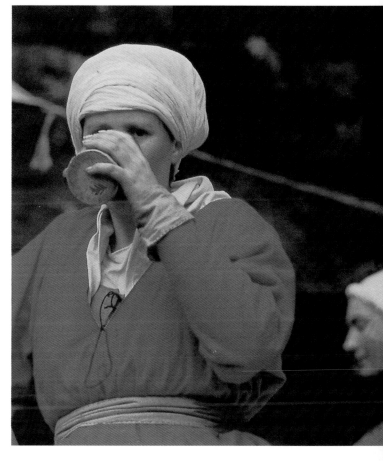

Many women played a very real part in the defence of castles and towns; young and robust, in desperate situations they knew that they were fighting for their lives. It is certain that arms and any available defensive clothing were sometimes handed out to women. Among many examples we read of the siege of Beauvais, France, by the Burgundians in 1472. Their attempts to take the town were only abandoned after a 25-day siege, a bombardment that demolished a quarter of the walls, and several failed assaults. The town was saved by its strong garrison of men-at-arms and archers, its townsmen and its womenfolk inspired by one Jeanne Hachette, emulating Joan of Arc. The women played such an important role in the defence that they were granted the right to wear whatever clothes they wished, and to precede their men in civic processions.

On the night of 19 July 1447 the German town of Soest was stormed: "...the armed citizens hurried to man the walls, and the women started to boil water and pitch under the wall-walks and to prepare tubs of quicklime." During the attack the besiegers' ladders turned out to be too short, so "the defensive measures that the women had prepared, namely pitch and quicklime that could be poured on the attackers to inflict burns, were particularly effective".

Enough similar descriptions survive to make it clear that women's participation in defence was the rule rather than the exception.

It is also clear that large numbers of women accompanied the armies, sometimes working in direct support of the military effort, sometimes actually fighting alongside the men. Some 4,000 from the Burgundian camp were once organised in an unsuccessful attempt to divert part of the Rhine. "These women", wrote an eyewitness, "were given a banner by the duke with a woman painted on it", and went to and fro "with banner, trumpets and pipes". There are examples of ladies of rank fighting fully armed in battle. In 1382 a woman was killed in battle in Flanders bearing the Flemings' banner, and in 1396 a Friesian woman "dressed in blue like a madwoman" fell pierced by arrows during a battle between Friesia and Hainault.

We read, following a defeat of the Burgundian army, that during their retreat "many women that were dressed in armour were struck down because they were unrecognised... many armed women, to protect their bodies and lives, exposed their breasts, proving that they were not men...". *(Photos: above Carlos Oliveira, far left John Howe, left Gerry Embleton)*

(Left) The Schilling chronicles often show women marching with the troops carrying canteens for the thirsty soldiers, or busy about the camp. *Cantinières* are drawn at the head of the marching column with the banners, fifes and drums. One wears a dress in cantonal colours, and clearly holds an officially recognised position. Twice women are shown armed with halbards; and once a woman is depicted as a member of a company of handgunners - she appears to carry her own gun, powder flask and bullet bag, and wears a red dress and the usual white headcloth and fringe.
(Photo John Howe)

(Below left) In Louis XI's time French master gunners were free to recruit what helpers they needed to man the guns, and on occasion are known to have enlisted their own wives. Here a member of a gunner's family fills cloth charge bags with powder from a large horn. Powder horns are shown carried by Swiss handgunners in the Schilling chronicles.
(Photo Carlos Oliveira)

(Below) A young woman helps with artillery equipment in camp; she will carry a water canteen for a Burgundian "field gun" crew - manning an artillery piece in summer weather is extremely thirsty work. The gun crew may be going into action and someone has lent her a livery jacket for identification in the smoke and confusion - though we have no evidence for this practice other than common sense.
(Photo John Howe)

The presence of large numbers of women in camp could, of course, lead to problems of discipline. Under Charles the Bold's ordinances of 1473 no more than 30 women were allowed to travel with each company on campaign, and none of them as "private property" - even so, there was trouble. At the siege of Neuss in 1474 English soldiers quarrelled over a wench and wanted to kill each other. The duke himself rushed to the spot to quell the trouble, but English archers "shot two or three times directly at him with their bows"; the arrows passed close by the unarmoured duke's head and shoulders, and his Burgundian soldiers, fearing assassination, rushed to attack the English mercenaries- this incident nearly caused a pitched battle.

(Above) A weary handgunner and his family rest beneath a rock during a long march through the forested hills of Alsace. This shows typical cold weather clothing as worn by soldiers and civilians alike; the men wear heavy woollen gowns, felt or wool hats and cloth mittens, the woman and child all that they have. This is the sort of scene which must have been repeated a hundred times at the tail of any army's column of march.

We have little specific information about the "tail" of medieval armies, but there is evidence that they were sometimes as large as those of the 17th century - which could equal the size of the active army. There was less restriction on personal entourages in medieval times - in fact they were an essential part of any nobleman's display of power and wealth. Valets, servants, cooks, musicians, priests, grooms, smiths, farriers, carters, and all *their* countless helpers, boys and women could be present as part of the "official" establishment. They might be joined by hordes of unofficial camp-followers - families, traders, craftsmen, prostitutes, refugees, hangers-on and opportunists of every kind, sprawling along behind the army. At times their numbers were strictly controlled and their behaviour regulated by a provost and his staff, but often not; their numbers hampered the army proper, and their scavenging aggravated the ruin visited on the surrounding countryside.
(Photos: above John Howe, left Gerry Embleton)

Religion
(Right & opposite)

The soldier's day, like that of the whole Christian world, was divided into three-hour periods by the canonical hours rung out on church or chapel bell. Most would pray on rising and before retiring, attend Mass on Sunday, and confess as often as piety prompted and opportunity allowed. A powerful undercurrent of shared faith, unsophisticated but very real flowed throughout Christendom.

The fear of the torments of Hell was actual and vivid, and it is clear that many were terrified of the judgement to come. The soldier may have pushed aside his sense of sin in the heat of battle and the face of temptation; but it was of great importance that priests be on hand to hear his confession and give absolution before battle, and to administer the last rites to the dying thereafter.

The Church, for all her faults, was probably friendlier to the poor and humble than any temporal power; and the best of her monks and priests embodied in their lives the sentiments written long years before by an English friar, Nicole Bozone: "At the day of judgement the simple folk will be exalted for their good deeds and the haughty abased for their pride. Then God will do as the mender of old clothes, who turns the lappet to the front, and what was uppermost downwards."

Yet while the power of the Church was universally respected, many of her representatives on earth had made themselves despised. The upkeep of churches and monasteries used up much of the money willed for "Christ's works"; and among the parish clergy were many who were ignorant of their offices and much given to worldly pleasures, forfeiting the respect of their flocks. While many good men and women did noble work in the name of charity, caring for the sick, the wounded and the destitute, 15th century bishops often lived the lives of heedless feudal rulers, enjoying ostentatious luxury and wielding immense political power - they were, after all, usually the younger brothers of the great rulers of the continent, cynically placed on an alternative ladder to riches. *(Photos Philippe Krauer/ L'Illustré Claude Huyghens & Françoise Danrigal)*

(Left) The soldiers of the Burgundian army described by an eyewitness before battle: "First, as is their usual custom, they made the sign of the cross on the ground and kissed it, and gave the war cry 'Notre Dame! Monseigneur St.Georges! Bourgogne!'..." No doubt many wore crosses or relics, and probably much older lucky charms as well, to be on the safe side.

(Above) The saints occupied an important place in the medieval world view, interceding between man and God, and their images on banners were popular talismans. Some carried by Burgundian units survive today in Swiss collections; this is a reconstruction of a 15th century banner of St.George - one can be sure that it was invested with far greater significance than simple unit identification by the soldiers who fought in its shadow. *(Photos Gerry Embleton)*

Priests at every level accompanied armies on campaign. It was not unusual for the great prince-bishops to actually lead troops into battle. In July 1447 the attack on the Westphalian Hanse city of Soest was led by the Bishop of Cologne, who took three arrow strikes on his helmet during an assault on the gates; while his ally the Bishop of Münster sank in the mud of the moat and had to be dragged out, swearing sulphurously, by his soldiers.

(Right & below) The humble priests who accompanied even small parties of soldiers must have varied widely in piety, learning, honesty and sobriety. No doubt some were greatly respected, even loved for their simple godliness, their ability to soothe a troubled man's soul and argue away his doubts; but many seem to have been despised as parasites who set no good example.

Apart from the care of souls, however, they had a practical function: although many military men could read and write a little, the priest was also often the clerk for the officers, the general book keeper for the company, and the letter writer for the soldiers. *(Photos: right Gerry Embleton, below Claude Huyghens & Françoise Danrigal, below inset Carlos Oliveira)*

Discipline

"...And when they had drunken enough of the wine that was in the taverns and other places, they full ungodly smote out the heads of the pipes and hogsheads of wine, that men went wet shod in wine, and then they robbed the town, and bare away bedding, cloth and other stuff, and befouled many women..." Thus an eyewitness on the Lancastrian army in Ludlow during the Wars of the Roses.

Normally a strict code of discipline was drawn up and published before a campaign, and more or less enforced during its course. Such codes were designed to protect the Church, women and children from robbery and maltreatment; they sometimes specifically included all non-combatants and private property, and laid out prices to be paid for food, the treatment of prisoners, and the arrangements for disposal of booty.

The punishments for desertion, cowardice and disobedience were often noted; they were usually harsh, and got harsher when conditions on campaign deteriorated - but commanders could on occasion be more lenient than those of two centuries later. Soldiers often enjoyed a measure of bargaining power, refusing to fight if not paid, demanding to air their grievances, and speaking up in support of accused comrades; it

sometimes paid a commander to tread lightly. We read of Charles the Bold addressing disgruntled English troops in their own language, mixing flattery with threats; but when pushed too hard he could lash about him with his sword, and order deserters put to death in a manner calculated to discourage any imitation.

Town levies - like those of Esslingen in 1476 - were threatened with fines, and banishment until they were paid, for any insubordination or cowardice. For a townsman banishment meant loss of livelihood and protection: outside his town he belonged nowhere, and might never be able to pay or return.

Such formal codes were, of course, as often honoured in the breech as the observance; individual wrongdoers might suffer their full rigour in a settled garrison or camp when there was time to bother about such things, but in more fluid circumstances soldiers might often plunder and murder with impunity, as long as they did not openly defy their commander or fail disgracefully in their duty to him.

After battle soldiers frequently got completely out of hand; towns that had to be taken by assault were given over to pillage and rape that could last for days at a time.

(Left) In 1475 Lübeck sent 600 men dressed in red and white to join the Imperial army, with 27 wagons painted red and white each bearing an individual device and the Imperial and Lübeck arms. Troops from Frankfurt travelled in their old uniforms until they arrived before the walls of Cologne, where they spent a whole weekend cleaning and polishing and then, in brand new uniforms, took part in the entry parade. The air fairly crackled with aggressive pride as various contingents rubbed shoulders; and serious quarrels broke out, resulting in casualties.

Westphalians, getting drunk "after their usual custom", fought the Bishop of Minister's men; and there were violent arguments over who should carry the Imperial and St.George's banners. An Imperial order was published forbidding the use of weapons - including, it was felt necessary to add, cannons! - against anyone other than the enemy; and instructing the contingents to take their beer and wine to their own tent-lines to drink, rather than boozing in dangerous proximity in the town streets. *(Photos John Howe)*

Troops were often a burden on the civil population; even in peacetime they stole, brawled, and bullied, and since they were often used as the instrument of oppression in a "police" role there was no love lost between soldier and civilian - particularly in the case of foreign mercenaries. Discipline seems always to have been difficult to enforce with anything approaching consistency, and even in well-regulated armies might go little further than the publication of an official code emphasised by the occasional exemplary punishment of a few individuals.
(Photos Gerry Embleton)

INTO BATTLE

There is no scope here for any detailed description of medieval tactics. (For a brilliant interpretation of the realities of combat we refer the reader to John Keegan's *The Face of Battle* - see Preface); but a few salient facts should be mentioned.

Opposing armies usually formed up in some sort of pre-arranged battle formation; there is no reason to suppose that these were much less sophisticated than those employed for the next three centuries, given that the missile troops enjoyed a range and rate of "fire" unsurpassed until the late 19th century. Some armies drew up with a vanguard, a main force, and some kind of rearguard or reserve. Cavalry were often placed on one or both flanks, and sometimes provided the reserve.

The main infantry blocks armed with pole weapons might provide the base, from whose protection missile men - archers, crossbow-

men, handgunners - could deploy, trying to disorder enemy formations and expose them to a decisive charge by armoured cavalry or polearm infantry. Alternatively, as in English armies, the main infantry line might be formed largely of archers interspersed with blocks of polearm infantry and mounted or dismounted men-at-arms. In this case the aim was to goad the enemy into advancing, to disorder his formations and cause havoc among his horses and unarmoured troops, and to so weaken them with archery that they could be defeated in hand-to-hand combat and by supporting cavalry charges when they finally managed to close. Most of the fighting might be on foot, knights and other men-at-arms frequently dismounting to fight among the footsoldiers; or it might include repeated cavalry charges.

Effective missile range was about 200-250 yards. Arrows lost their force beyond this range, and armour gave good protection; but only a relatively small proportion of any army wore full armour, and cavalry horses were seldom protected. It was important for the attackers to close with the

defenders, to get out of the killing-ground swept by arrows and shot and within the effective range of the attackers' weapons.

Most combat was hand-to-hand with blade and point: after shuffling forward under the lash of arrows and gunshot, unable to see anything but the backs of the men in front and crammed together by the press of bodies all around, the soldiers who reached the enemy line hacked and stabbed in savage desperation. Unless one side fell back before actual contact, or one side quickly broke the other's weakened ranks, then the advance would grind to a bloody halt. No matter how deep the formations, only the front rank or two of each force could actually fight at any given moment - thrusting, cutting, swaying, jostling, stumbling, hesitating until a man fell and a gap appeared which one or two brave attackers might exploit...

Very often the armies would be formed up in several self-contained masses. When one was broken the attackers would advance on the next, perhaps to be broken in their turn. Once battle was joined there was seldom opportunity for senior commanders to exercise any tactical control beyond the bodies of troops under their immediate leadership. It was the sort of combat that could degenerate into one great charnel-house; or in which victory or defeat could turn on the behaviour of a single part of

the army - the berserker example that sent a thrill of confidence through the close-packed mass, or the weak link whose collapse broke the chain.

The two armies might draw apart, bloody and exhausted, to fight another day. If one side broke before too long and fled the field the victors might press forward in pursuit, butchering the fleeing mob without mercy. At other times the winners might remain on the field, too weary or disorganised for pursuit, too cautious to risk counter-attack or ambush - or, often, too intent on looting the enemy's camp. (The Swiss seem often to have followed an ancient custom whereby the "legitimacy" of a victory depended on their occupying the field for three days. They seldom followed and destroyed their enemy - but usually took no prisoners; and were much occupied with sharing out whatever booty had been taken.)

Prisoners might be ransomed; made to swear allegiance to a new prince; allowed to make their way home; or murdered, sometimes with great cruelty. (Italian mercenaries captured by the Swiss during the Burgundian wars were accused of every possible crime, and burned alive in the city of Basle.)
(Photos: left John Howe, above Gerry Embleton)

Some writers of the 14th to 16th centuries, on battle:

"I love to see a lord when he is the first to advance on horseback, armed and fearless, thus encouraging his men to valiant service; then, when the fray has begun, each must be ready to follow him willingly, because no one is held in esteem until he has given and received blows. We shall see clubs and swords, gaily coloured helmets and shields shattered and spoiled...and many vassals all together receiving great blows, by reason of which many horses will wander riderless.... Once he has started fighting no noble knight thinks of anything but breaking heads and arms – better a dead man than a live one who is useless. I tell you, neither in eating, drinking nor sleeping do I find what I feel when I hear the shout 'At them!' from both sides, and the neighing of riderless horses in the confusion, or the cry 'Help! Help!', or when I see great and small fall on the grass of the ditches, or when I espy dead men who still have pennoned lances in their ribs." (Bertrand de Born)

"It is a joyous thing, a war. You love your comrade so much in war. When you see that your quarrel is just, and your blood is fighting well, tears rise to your eyes. A great sweet feeling of loyalty and of pity fills your heart on seeing your friend so valiantly exposing his body. And then you are prepared to go and die or live with him, and for love not to abandon him. And out of that there arises such a delight, that he who has not experienced it is not fit to say what delight is. Do you think that a man who does that fears death? Not at all, for he feels so strengthened, so elated, that he does not know where he is. Truly he is afraid of nothing."
(Jean de Bevil)

"The crossbow quarrels fell like rain, the clouds hung low, and the air was thick with dust...the Aretina infantry, knife in hand, crawled under the bellies of the horses and disembowelled them..."
(Florentine chronicle, 1311-12)

"We'll move against the enemy until the very women and little children cry 'Murder!'– that is what we long for and joy in!"
(Niklaus Manuel, 1515)

"When two nobles quarrel, the poor man's thatch goes up in flames..." (Anon)

(Photos: above & right, John Howe; pages 126-127, John Howe; pages 128-129, Gerry Embleton, inset John Howe)

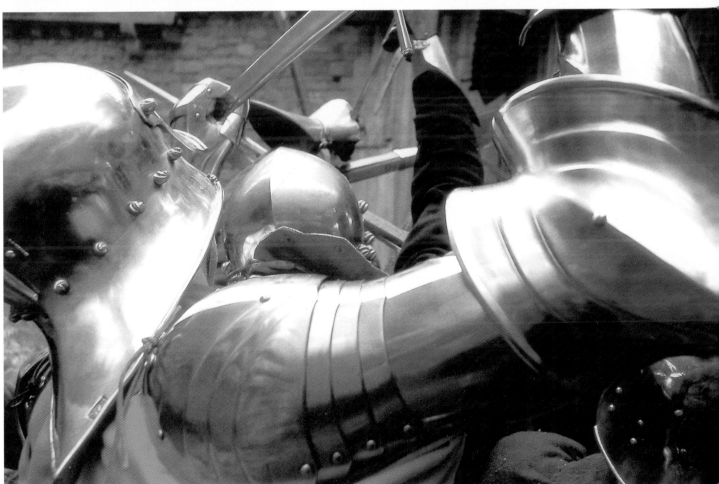

Winter campaigns

Although the summer months were preferred for campaigning, military leaders did not hesitate to make war in winter if it served their purpose. Great sieges continued under harsh winter conditions, and raids and campaigns were launched despite severe hardship.

During the Wars of the Roses Queen Margaret's hardy northern troops swept south in the depth of the winter of 1461. "They robbed, despoiled and devastated and carried off with them whatever they could come upon or discover, whether garments or money, herds or cattle or single animals, sparing neither churches nor clergy..."

In 1464 Charles the Bold led a punishment raid against the castle and town of Franchimont in terrible winter weather. Some of his men suffered frostbite, "so that their toenails came out and they suffered much from hunger, thirst and cold." De Commynes relates how frozen wine was hacked out of the barrels with an axe and carried away in baskets or hats.

A Swiss chronicler describes the battle of Nancy, 5 January 1477: "And now the God-fearing Confederates and other men that were there heard the Burgundians shouting, and when they saw and realised that the guns were being turned on them they waited no longer, and ran quickly down the hill and through a thick hedge. One of Lucerne, named Küri Köit, arrived on his horse in the midst of the enemy before the rest of the army. He was carrying a small pennon, and was rushed by the Burgundians. who thought he was a proper ensign. He had an uncontrollable horse, and was therefore brought down and killed. God save his soul, for he died in a knightly manner. Many people were also brought down at the hedge by longbow arrows. However, the pressure was so great that the hedge was flattened, and through God's help the Burgundians were put to flight..." *(Photo Carlos Oliveira)*

Death of a soldier

Sir John Bourchier (c. 1469–1533) describes the death in a skirmish of the 14th century English hero Sir John Chandos, a veteran of Crécy, Poitiers and Najara:

"The same morning there had fallen a great dew so that the ground was somewhat moist, and so in his going forward he slid and fell down at the joining of his enemies and as he was arising there light a stroke on him given by a squire called Jakes of Sant Martin with his glaive the which stroke entered into the flesh under his eye between the nose and the forehead. Sir John Chandos saw not the stroke coming on that side for he was blind in one eye. He lost the sight thereof a five year before as he hunted after an hart in the lands of Bordeaux. And also he had on no visor. The stroke was rude and entered into his brain the which stroke grieved him so sore that he overthrew on the earth and turned for pain two time upside down as he that was wounded to death, for after that stroke he never spoke word..."

Defeat, and aftermath

The army of the Swiss lifted the siege of Murten on 22 June 1476, overrunning the Burgundian camp despite heavy artillery fire:

"...More than one soldier was shot apart on that day, and not a few had their heads shot off...". The enemy guns were taken and "many of the gun-masters cut down at their guns". In total confusion, the larger part of the Burgundian army was pinned against the lake shore and butchered. "Those who ran into the lake were drowned as they stood up to their necks in the water.... Many climbed into trees in a village near Murten called Faoug, from which they were speared or shot down like squirrels. Many also hid their heads in ovens or in the bushes and were killed by being stabbed in their behinds" - not a callous dramatisation, but an accurate description of behaviour observed in modern war, when cornered, demoralised soldiers hide in their sleeping bags, unable to face the horror of what is about to happen to them.

A broken army were vulnerable to all, and every man's hand was against them; country folk turned out to slaughter lone fugitives, for vengeance, robbery – or simply to enjoy, for once in a lifetime, power over a soldier. After the Burgundian defeat at Nancy the chronicles describe the roads littered with the corpses of those killed and stripped by the peasants.

Desperate, frost-bitten fugitives arrived before the locked gates of Metz in the early hours of the morning, and threw themselves into the snow-filled moat, crying out to the watchmen "in the name of God's holy passion" to be let in. The guard commander was called from his bed and interrogated them; we may imagine him and his guards, wrapped in their cloaks in a pool of lantern light, shouting their questions down into the darkness. Unsatisfied, he dismissed the huddled figures below as rogues, and went back to bed. Some time later the watch reported the moat full of people, crying out desperately; this time one voice was recognised, and the gates were opened. The news of the defeat and death of Duke Charles was not at first believed, but the townsfolk did what they could for the poor wretches. Some 140 to 160 died in the great hospital of St. Nicolas at Le Neufbourg from wounds, and cold.

(Left & below)
De Commynes, writing of the Wars of the Roses:

"It is the custom of the English that, once they have gained a battle, they do no more killing, especially killing of common people; for each side seeks to please the commons.... King Edward told me that in all the battles he had won, the moment he came to victory he mounted a horse and shouted that the commons were to be spared and the nobles slain. And of the latter, few or none escaped.... The realm of England enjoys one favour above all other realms, that neither the countryside nor the people are destroyed nor are buildings burnt or demolished. Misfortune falls on soldiers and nobles in particular...." It has been calculated that of the noble families in England before the Wars of the Roses, just over 25 per cent were extinct by 1485.
(Photos Gerry Embleton; inset Paul Knight)

Death and Wounds

"...And with them many of their followers wounded, mostly in the face and lower half of the body, a very pitiable sight. May God preserve them.... Those who set out with good horses and sound bodies returned home with sorry nags and bandaged races, some without noses etc. and preferred to stay indoors. May God have pity at this wretched spectacle, for it is said that there had been no fiercer battle in England for the last 100 years than happened last Easter as I have described, may God henceforth give us his eternal peace." (Gerhard von Wesel, a Hanseatic merchant, on the aftermath of the battle of Barnet, 14 April 1471.)

It is almost impossible to discover the true number of casualties for any medieval battle. The records, if kept accurately, have seldom survived; and it was usual for chroniclers to exaggerate for propaganda purposes, sometimes grossly - occasionally the reported casualties outnumbered the known total present.

It does not take much imagination to be horrified by the thought of the wounds inflicted by medieval weapons in hand-to-hand fighting. Eloquent witnesses were unearthed, in great numbers, from mass graves at Wisby on the Swedish island of Gotland, site of a battle in 1361. The skeletal remains of some 1,185 men were recovered; their slashed and pierced flesh had long withered away, but their bones bore mute testimony to the effectiveness of blade and point. Many shins are notched and hacked - the legs were vulnerable to a disabling cut while the soldier concentrated on defending head and torso; one skeleton has both legs severed by a single great blow. Skulls and mail coifs are pierced and broken, and heads split to the teeth. Crossbow bolts have left square holes punched into the bones; some skulls still have bolt heads lodged in them, and more than one shows an exit wound where a bolt has passed clean through the skull - an appalling indication of their power. The grouping of cuts suggests that as soon as a man gained an advantage he rained repeated blows on his reeling opponent, often finishing him off as he lay helpless.

Sword and dagger, polearm and mace, cannon and handgun shot, arrow and bolt produced much the same sort of wounds as their 18th and 19th century counter-parts, though often more massive. Bills and halliards inflicted crushing and cutting wounds, smashing heads and severing limbs; enormous gashes bled the wounded to death; arrows pierced deep, carrying in fragments of filthy cloth and rusty iron.

Medical care

Some of our ancestors managed to survive nightmare wounds; military surgeons gained great practical experience, but could do little or nothing against infection and gangrene.

University-trained physicians and surgeons were rare, and the knowledge and skill of most practicioners varied enormously. A certain amount of basic education was necessary to understand medical textbooks; and guilds like that of the Barber-Surgeons in London battled against the large numbers of quack "leeches" and unskilled barbers who maimed rather than cured their patients.

We have certainly progressed hugely over the past 150 years in the treatment of infections, the use of antibiotics, and many other fields of medecine; but we should not dismiss medieval methods utterly. Working rather like modem homeopathic practitioners, balancing the elements and "humours" in the body, some 15th century doctors were probably sound pragmatic diagnosticians. Some of the herbal medicines they used were surprisingly successful; others were useless or harmful, the recipes recalling Macbeth's witches. Many sensible ideas were imported from the Arab world; and as every housewife had to be her own family doctor, and many religious houses provided hospitals, a good deal of practical knowledge was passed down the generations. However, the pernicious practice of bleeding - and therefore further weakening the patient - was widespread, as it would remain almost into modem times.

John Ardenne was surgeon to Henry Plantagenet, Earl of Derby and later Duke of Lancaster in the second half of the 14th century. In the 1370s he wrote a surgical treatise which was still used during the following century. An experienced practical surgeon, his works sometimes reveal a surprisingly "modem" approach. He invented a procedure for the treatment of fistula still employed, in its essentials, today. He taught that wounds should heal without suppuration, and that dressings should be infrequent and should not irritate.

(Photos: above John Howe, right Gerry Embleton)

There were surgeons and physicians accompanying the armies, but very few: just nine, for instance, were present at the siege of Berwick in 1482 under command of the king's surgeon William Hobbes.

No doubt there were many amateur healers among the soldiers; with a country man's knowledge of common injuries and remedies; and charitable civilian populations and religious houses did their best to help the wounded soldier lucky enough to reach their care. If a casualty could be taken swiftly to a "hospital" he might be well cared for by the standards of the day; but in general the recovery of the common soldier wounded in battle or diseased in the camp must have been as much of a lottery as it remained in the 18th century.

At Bijloke hospital in Ghent during the war years 1488-92. "...we were so overwhelmed by the sick that two or three of them always had to lie together in one bed. Within these five years more than 2,000 patients died..."

There was a horrendous remedy for black-powder burns which involved the excrement of wild boars; but severe burns were usually beyond the skills of a 15th century doctor. The gravely wounded soldier could only hope for a different cure for his sufferings. Early in the next century a doctor with the French army entering Milan saw three casualties suffering from terrible powder burns. An old soldier asked him if he could do anything for them; and when the doctor replied that he could not, the veteran gently cut their throats. To the enraged doctor he replied "...that he prayed to God that when he should be in such a state he might find someone who would do the same for him, to the end that he might not languish miserably." *(Photo John Howe)*

(Right) A beautifully reconstructed set of surgeon's tools and knives in a carrying case, along with saws and tourniquets the most frequently used implements of the field surgeon. *(Photo John Howe)*

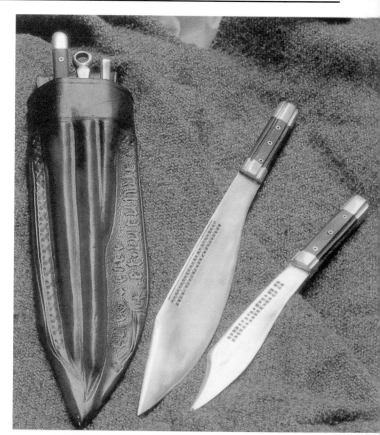

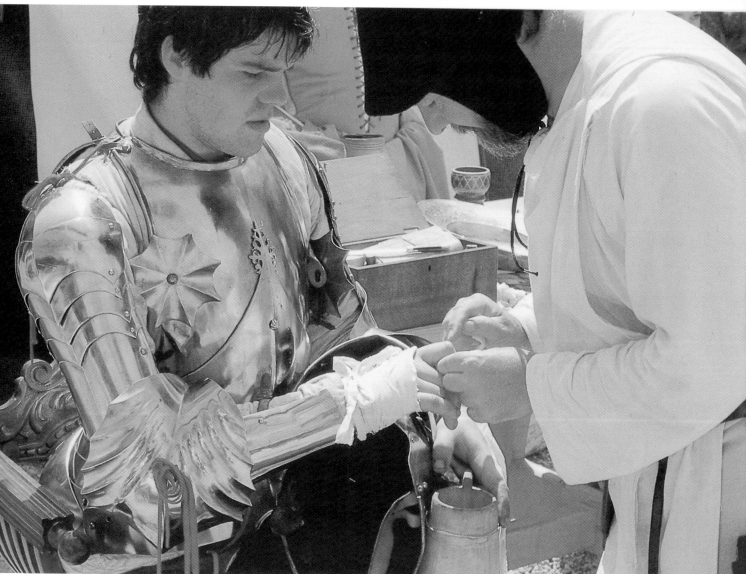

(Above) Guillebert de Lannoy, 1412: "...We retreated into the castle... but... they only set fire to the town and went oft with their booty, and I was wounded in the thigh by a vireton [crossbow bolt] between my armour and I carried its point in my thigh for more than nine months..." *(Photo Carlos Oliveira)*

(Left) Whenever possible the dead - or at least, those of the winning army - were buried in sanctified ground, but this depended on time, mood and circumstance. Bodies might be carried away or buried by their friends; burned; thrown into great pits; tipped into the nearest river, or simply left to rot in the woods. Many were buried by the owners of the land on which they lay. A monument might be set up, like the chapel of Notre Dame de Talbot erected by French captains on the battlefield of Castillon to honour their fallen enemy. A cross with an inscription, or a simple mound, might mark a mass grave until time and nature erased it, leaving the dead to sleep overgrown and forgotten. Masses might be said for the souls of the high-born, their names being recorded on a roll of honour by some conscientious chronicler. The common soldiers who fell remain, for the most part, nameless. Normally the dead were stripped, and anything valuable or usable was taken by the possessors of the battlefield or the scavengers who came out to haunt it. *(Photo Gerry Embleton)*

Booty

The chance of plunder was certainly one of the most attractive inducements to follow a soldier's life. Sometimes regulations ordered that everything captured should be handed in, to be shared out fairly; but many soldiers sold their loot on the spot, or to the first merchant or trader they could find. Rather like 18th century sailors, some made enough "prize money" to set themselves up in a shop, to marry well, or to pay off family debts; but most were as poor at the end of a campaign as they had been the day it began.

The Swiss were very much occupied with the question of plunder; elaborate regulations for the division of any spoils were drawn up before a campaign. Veteran Swiss troops under Hans Waldmann of Zürich and Brand von Stein, passing through Alsace on their way to Nancy in the late 1470s, amused themselves by savagely attacking Jews en route and sending all their valuables to Berne.

The Swiss cantons made unusual profits out of their wars with Burgundy, particularly after they looted the Burgundian camp – a travelling royal court – at Grandson in 1476. Schilling wrote:
"Everyone who had captured a piece was required to put it in the common collection, so that everyone would receive the same amount and the distribution would be done in a communal and fair way. However, those who had captured booty also tended to keep it. If this distribution was carried out in an honest way, I cannot tell, but many who had been very poor before the battle came afterwards to great wealth, so that they and theirs have been able to keep better houses up to the present day."

By the time the clerks tried to make an inventory of each soldier's loot many absent-minded or careless warriors turned out to have "lost", "lent" or "sold" their plunder, or to have "bought" their new possessions, or taken them in fair-exchange for their own lost gear; and we can read the lists of excuses today, the names of families and villages still recognisable: "Fridlij Pfister has ostrich feathers, he lost an armour.... Heini Elsser has bought a horse and a silk gown and has a crossbow, but he lost a horse and also his belt and a little purse with money, a dagger and a coat.... Hans von Bruck from Ebikon has a pair of hose which he is wearing and a gilded paternoster which he bought...he lost his pike during the fighting.... Hans Krebsser has nothing but two sets of playing cards...". We also read of "Gretlij, in the house of women", and "Anna from Zürich, a travelling lady", who each got a share alongside the soldiers whose company they kept. *(Photos Gerry Embleton)*

(Below)
"The war is over...Where shall we go now?" - Hans Sebald Beham, 1543.

After the war the townsman or farmer-soldier might return to his home, if it were still standing, the lucky few richer than when they left. Some of the younger men may have got a taste for the soldier's life, and followed the mercenary bands to the next campaign. Others found employment in the retinue of some lord; or turned to banditry, taking part in the scramble for scraps of territory or property that followed a war. Many - the sick and injured, their health broken by wounds or disease - joined the shadowy army of the dispossessed, surviving as best they could on the charity of the less unfortunate.

(Photo Philippe Krauer/ L'Illustr'e)

Charity

Poor relief functioned erratically. Money, food and clothing were sometimes distributed to the needy, more generously if the economic prospects were improving and the unemployed might be needed again soon. Each village or town had its own elderly or destitute to care for. In bad times - as was usually the case in the aftermath of war - the local authorities might treat their own poor more harshly, so as to discourage any influx of refugees from the countryside round about. Disabled or desperate ex-soldiers were rarely welcome anywhere; begging or stealing was their only hope.

In Burgundy in the 1450S-60S the town poor relief institution, "The Table of the Holy Spirit", issued a metal token to be worn by the acceptable poor - those without it were turned away. All healthy men were forced to find jobs, or to serve in the galleys. Many hospitals existed, originally associated with various religious institutions and primarily concerned with helping the sick and the penniless. But as richer patients bequeathed a proportion of their estates, or turned over their fortunes while living in return for a comfortable and secure old age in the hospitals, these changed in character, becoming more elitist. Some were arranged like groups of almshouses, around a central court and common facilities; others, like St. John's in Bruges, had one massive ward with room for more than 100 patients (where contagious diseases ran riot).

Although a reasonably well-to-do disabled soldier might find a comfortable retirement in one of these institutions, there was little or no place there for the common archer or pikeman.

(Photo above: Gerry Embleton)

The petition of Thomas Hostelle, 1429:
"To the King our sovereign Lord. Beseecheth meekly your poor liegeman and humble petitioner, Thomas Hostelle, that, in consideration of his service done in your noble progenitors time...being at the siege of Harfleur thare smitten with a quarrel through the head losing one eye and his cheek bone broken, also at the battle of Agincourt, and before at the taking of the Carracks at Sea, there a gadde of iron his plates smitten into his body and his hand smitten in sunder, and sore hurt, maimed and wounded, by mean whereof he being sorely feebled and debrused, now falle to great age and poverty..."
(Photo John Howe)

ACKNOWLEDGEMENTS

This book has been a true team effort; sadly, there is not space to thank by name everyone whose kindness, helpfulness and support has carried the project along over the last seven years, nor to describe their contributions in detail.

We are sure that all will understand if we start by mentioning collectively the members of the Company of Saynte George, who figure in most of the photographs, and whose patience in sun, rain and snow, whose goodwill and humour, and whose high standards of costume, equipment and general attitude to "living history" have made the book possible. The Company tries to bring to life a small 15th century Burgundian company in garrison and camp. It does not "re-enact" battles, and most of the scenes in this book have been set up and posed as they would be for a film. The Company strives to preserve a comradely atmosphere mixing very hard work, strict discipline, and an irrepressible sense of humour. Membership is by invitation, but close and friendly co-operation with other groups is part of Company policy.

Our sincere and grateful thanks to the members of Wolfbane, The White Company, The Black Prince's Household and 1471, for their generous hospitality and welcome, and for allowing us to interrupt their weekends.

We wish to express our gratitude to the curators and staff of the many museums and castles that have generously opened their doors to us.

In Switzerland, to the Château de Chillon; Historical Museum Lucerne; Historical Museum Lausanne; particular thanks to Mme.J.Ehrenburg of the Château de Grandson for many kindnesses over the years; and to Dr.Hans Dürst, formerly director of Schloss Lenzburg, who literally gave us the key to the castle, and generously backed our experiments. In Germany: to the Stuttgart Historical Museum, and Herr Kaiser of Wäscherschloss. In France, to the Château de Haute-Koenigsbourg in Alsace; and the organisers of the festival "Le Roi de l'Oiseau" in Le Puy-en-Velay for their warm friendship, and the unique chance they gave us to develop our ideas in the field. Thanks to costumiers Caroline Thorpe, Marina Harrington and especially to Angela Lowes and Keith Bartlett, who have taught us a lot.

To Dani Geser for all his enthusiasm and ideas; to Simon Metcalfe, Will Hutt, Walter Suckert, Sue Githens, Boesch of Yverdon, and Gilbert Chabloz for their special contributions. To Ian Ashdown, who has generously shared his unparalleled knowledge and practical experience of arms and armour over the years; to Renato Paccozzi for his many kindnesses; and to Paul Gerber for the boar...

To Nick Michael, John Richards, Hartmut Writh and Clive Bartlett for letting us use their material and translations. To a private collector who allowed me to study and handle his wonderful collection of arms and armour over ten years....

To Monique Flood for her typing; and to Anne Embleton-Perret for her encouragement, typing and translations of both French and German and the author's appalling manuscript.

Our thanks to Martin Windrow for his encouragement, and for letting us have a shot at it.

Lastly but certainly not least, we would like to thank the photographers who have generously allowed us to use their pictures, without which this book would be a shadow of itself: Anik Diserans, Françoise Danrigal and Claude Huyghens, Anne Embleton-Perret, Philippe Krauer of *L'Illustr'e* magazine, Simon Metcalfe, Carlos Oliveira, Suzanne Hupfer, Alan and Michael Perry, Hans Weber, Gillian Brooks, Ian Ashdown, Robert Hoare of Wolfbane, Martin Render, David Gallagher, and Paul Knight.

(Above) The Company of St.George's tented camp in the courtyard of Lenzburg Castle in Switzerland. The Company has occupied the castle as its garrison on two occasions, and was there in 1991 during the celebrations of Switzerland's 700th anniversary.
(Photo Hans Weber)

(Left) The master-gunner instructs a party of ladies in the mysteries of his black art.
(Photo Hans Weber)

(Above right) The Company's sword-master, as jovial as ever, with one lady admirer and one deeply suspicious young recruit.
(Photo Martin Render)

(Right) This beautifully set-up photograph shows members of the Company devouring the wild boar shown on page 113 - one of the "perks" of staging realistic hunting scenes.
(Photo Philippe Krauer/L'Illustr'e)

The authors Gerry Embleton (seated) and John Howe (standing right) discuss with other members a terribly serious point of research. Another member, at right, is absorbed in making a model Kon-Tiki raft from straw for an evening entertainment – an all-classes boat race across the castle fishpond, which involved the expenditure of quantities of gunpowder, and after which the term "stockfish" acquired an entirely new resonance for all ranks.... This neatly illustrates the two sides of the Company of Saynte George.
(Photo Hans Weber)

The Company has an unusually high proportion of members who work in or for museums or in related fields, but otherwise recruits members of both sexes from all walks of life. Members' ages range from six months to dignified. We seriously research, reconstruct and experiment with costume, tools, utensils, weapons, techniques, and many items in everyday use in the 1470s. For further information please contact:
The Company of Saynte George
c/o Time Machine
1425 Onnens
Switzerland